MW00657675

Shadow Chaser
The In-Between

Sean Austin
with David Weatherly

Shadow Chaser
The In-Between

by Sean Austin with David Weatherly

Some names have been changed to protect the privacy of those involved.

ISBN: 978-1-945950-20-9 (Paperback)

Published by

Eerie Lights Publishing
Eerielightspublishing.com

Cover art by Sam Shearon
www.mister-sam.com

Original art by Kimberly Carper

Borg's Woods and Amityville photos by Kamra Images

Edited by "b"

Layout by SMAK
www.smakgraphics.com

Printed in the United States of America

Table of Contents

Introduction

It is hard to believe that I am sitting here writing this, the introduction to my second book. Thanks to all of you who have supported my journey this far and have asked for more.

I am also thankful to God and to the spirits who have communicated with me as I continue my work. Without their cooperation, I would not be able to continue doing what I do.

Despite the fact that I have many paranormal investigations under my belt now, I am still frequently amazed at what happens at many locations. The constant amazement and desire to help are two of the biggest driving factors that keep me passionate about the field and help me continue, even when things are challenging or difficult. I am always willing to help any spirits that are present at a location. I do this primarily by prayer, focusing on blessings and white light, and trying my best to connect them to God.

Often, I try to help spirits by letting them know it is okay to go into the light of God's love. It is amazing to me that many times when I say a prayer for those who are stuck, I hear the word "prayer" repeated over various devices, or sometimes with my psychic senses.

The notion that I can help, or really the notion that any human can help someone stuck as a ghost, may seem to be a stretch, but, after all, we are all here to help each other. I believe this holds true whether those involved have a physical body or are in a ghostly form.

For many years now, I have had visions, powerful psychic dreams, and have heard things clairaudiently. As I have continued my work in the paranormal field, I have learned there are some personal symbols that tell me things during the work I do.

For instance, I have come to understand that when I see the image or vision of a white dove, it is symbolic of a female spirit crossing over. As these symbols and my gifts have become more refined, I have been guided to incorporate more and more into my methods. One common practice I utilize involves the use of visualizing white light while praying. I offer this method here in the event that it may help some readers with their own processes.

To start, I close my eyes while I envision white light coming down. I believe the combination of visualization and faith is very powerful, so, as I envision this light, I recite a prayer. There are two traditional Catholic prayers that I say as I continuously keep envisioning this bright, white light. Here are the prayers I use:

Our Father, Who art in Heaven,
Hallowed be Thy Name.
Thy Kingdom come,
Thy will be done,
On earth, as it is in Heaven.
Give us this day our daily bread
And forgive us our trespasses
As we forgive those who trespass against us,
And lead us not into temptation,
But deliver us from evil.
For the Kingdom
The power and the glory are yours
Now and forever.
Amen

Hail Mary,
Full of Grace,
The Lord is with thee
Blessed art though among women,
And blessed is the fruit
Of thy womb, Jesus.
Holy Mary,
Mother of God,
Pray for us sinners now,
And at the hour of our death.

I am sure these prayers will be familiar to many of you. They have been around for a very long time and with good reason—they are effective for many spiritual people and can be used in any situation to call on the grace and power of God and heavenly forces.

Another piece that I utilize is a prayer that incorporates the Archangel Michael. Now, let me be clear; I cannot force earthbound spirits to cross over, none of us can. But sometimes an extra push can go a long way in giving them an extra incentive to accept God's unconditional love and forgiveness. To me, it is like handing them a flashlight to use in a darkened room, giving them the courage to move forward and find the way out.

Letting go of human bounds and attachments isn't always easy for some souls, so by directing these words specifically, with the right intent, it can give them what they need to break free. I've, personally, seen some remarkable evidence to show that this works. Here's the Archangel Michael prayer I use:

I pray to you, Archangel Michael,
To bring down the white light of the Holy Spirit
And let any souls here willing to accept God's
Unconditional love and forgiveness
To go towards the light and bring their loved ones
To the light to give them
Extra incentive and courage to do so
I ask this through Christ, our Lord.
Amen

After I say this prayer, I bless myself with the cross of the Father, Son, and Holy Spirit. I started using this method a long time ago and still use it to this day. I've found it very effective in my work, and there seems to be no end to the positive outcomes.

Frequently, I receive evidence from spirits that further

confirms the effectiveness of this method. It's amazing how many times I have heard them say "pray," "prayer," and "thank you" when using this approach.

You see, often when I'm doing an investigation and encounter spirits that need help, I leave a ghost box running as a way for them to communicate. This gives the spirits yet another outlet and often backs up my own intuitions and visions that I receive. I've also heard responses from spirits telling me that they are free and are leaving to go into the light. It's always a joyous thing to have such confirmations.

Of course, there is the other side, too. I find that saying these prayers when malevolent spirits are present creates a whole range of responses, mostly anger, rage, and vile words and curses. Trying to help lost souls angers the demons and devils that lurk at many haunted locations, and my work often leads to confrontations. Frequently, these dark entities will try to attack me and stop my work any way they can.

This book will cover some dark cases that I have been involved with and hopefully give you an idea of some of the evil things that can be encountered when walking a path of spiritual work in the paranormal.

The Infiltration

There's a story that I've wanted to tell for some time. It's the account of a case I was involved with over a long period of time when I was still a novice in the field of demonology.

In many ways, it was a crash course in dealing with true evil. Once I found myself in the midst of it, I learned there was no turning back. I also learned the depths to which demonic forces will go when someone becomes the target of their attention.

In a roundabout way, the case started with, of all things, a paranormal app. Now, if you're a paranormal investigator reading this, I know that you're likely rolling your eyes and thinking, "Those things are phony!" or, "Those don't work for genuine investigations." Everyone is entitled to their opinion but let me just share my own perspective and experience on this matter.

When I got into the paranormal, I was looking at whatever tools I could find to help me investigate. I had just gotten an iPhone and I was looking for paranormal apps. I'd heard there were several available that people were using with various results. I came across one called Ghost Radar. Honestly, yeah, I thought it was a joke myself, but hey, I had a new smartphone, and here was an app that had to do with the paranormal. It didn't cost anything to try it out.

I was in the attic of my old apartment, sitting back, watching TV with my sister, and playing with this Ghost Radar. The app has a little "radar" screen that is supposed to indicate when ghosts are around, and there's a verbal component that gives random words.

I was sitting there with this app running while I was talking to my sister. I mentioned to her that a friend down the street had tragically taken his own life. "I wonder if his spirit is still around," I said.

The first word I ever heard out of this application gave both my sister and me the chills because it said our friend's name. Now, let me emphasize a couple of things here. I had only said my friend's first name when speaking to my sister, but the app mentioned both his first and last name. His last name is pretty unique. For me, this was mind-blowing.

When I researched the app online, I found that hundreds of other people were having unique experiences with this app, things that simply were not explainable by a pre-programmed app. I started to believe there was more to the app than skeptical investigators thought possible.

I, personally, believe that spirits are able to manipulate anything that uses electrical energy. Over time, I've had many correlations between this simple app and my own psychic abilities. For me, it's undeniable, and it's one of those things that just can't be explained away easily.

Now, I know I've gone on a bit of a tangent, but this does come around to the case in question—I'm getting there.

Sometimes paranormal cases can come to you in funny ways. When I was working on my first book, I was hanging out with my buddy, Gregory, one day. Honestly, we were both pretty hungover from the previous night, and we were joking around about all kinds of stuff, the paranormal included. Somehow, we got started on the Ghost Radar, joking about how it was a silly name. We started saying the name over and over in a funny voice, and it led to writing down lyrics to a song about the app.

Before the paranormal, music was my first passion, and it still remains a driving force in my life, so this kind of thing wasn't too unusual for me. Granted, it was done as a joke, but I thought it was pretty good and ended up recording a little demo of it on my phone. I decided to send it to the creator of the app, making it clear that I actually did enjoy the app, and that I used it, but that I was also a musician and thought the song was pretty fun.

The response was unexpected. The app's creator contacted me back and hired me to record the song professionally for the app. It was a crazy turn of events, but the song was an unexpected hit, breaking into the top hundred on iTunes, and it was big in thirteen different countries! People even did parodies of the song on YouTube. Because of this attention, other people interested in the paranormal started finding me and contacting me. One of these individuals was a girl named Abby.

Abby messaged me, asking about an incident involving some scratches that manifested on my friend, Gregory when he and I were doing an investigation. She had read my posting on the Unexplained Mysteries site about the incident and explained how she had experienced something similar. She knew I was an investigator and hoped to find some answers that would explain her own experiences. Little did I know what those experiences would entail.

Abby sent me a photo of the scratches she had received. They were huge! I couldn't believe how obvious and pronounced they were. In talking with her, I learned that Abby had messed around with witchcraft and that after she had done so, she began to have weird experiences.

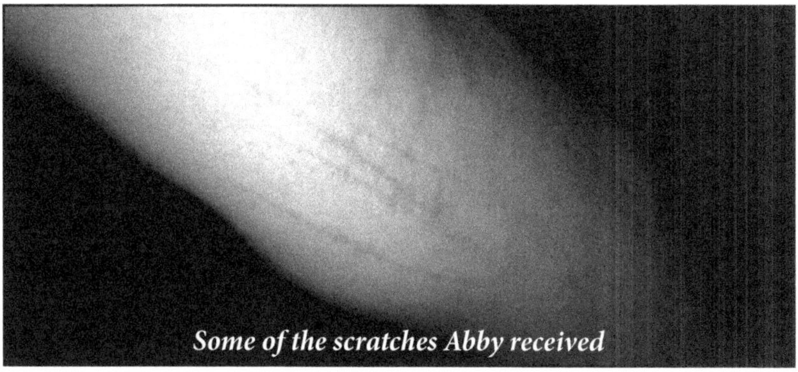

Some of the scratches Abby received

I told Abby that dabbling in such things was a bad idea and that such practices could open the door for a lot of entities and dark influences to come in. I explained to her that I use my faith as protection against demons and negative entities. This was still early on in my experience as an investigator, and I told Abby that there were things I was still learning myself, but I gave her the warnings, hoping that it would offer her some guidance and help with what she was experiencing.

It was a couple of years later before I talked to Abby again. Out of nowhere, she sent me a frantic message. She was in trouble and needed help. She told me that whatever she had been dealing with before wasn't that bad overall, but now she was pregnant with her second child, and the activity around her had increased dramatically. She didn't know what to do or who to turn to for help, and she was really scared.

I had gone through a lot of lessons on my path at that point, and there had been a recurring theme for me being called to these kinds of situations. Of course, these were challenging situations, and I never knew exactly what was coming or how dark the situation might be. But again, if someone needed help and I could do something, I was certainly going to try.

I started having conversations with Abby on the phone, learning all I could about the situation and what she was experiencing, what kinds of manifestations were taking place, and what effects they were having on her. There was a long list of strange things happening to this woman.

She was having nightmares on a regular basis, and while this was something that was both disturbing and concerning, there was another, more alarming condition that had manifested. She was losing track of time.

I asked her to explain this more carefully and define what she meant. She said that she was slipping into some kind of trance state and that afterwards, she wouldn't remember what had occurred while she was out. She would snap out of the trance state and realize that something strange had happened, but she couldn't understand why it was occurring.

Adding to the disturbing nature of these incidents, she

discovered that there would be scratches on her body when she came out of the trance. AND, if that wasn't creepy enough, she also discovered writing and what appeared to be witchcraft symbols on a nearby mirror. At one point, she came out of the trance to find the symbols and the name Issabella written on the mirror.

Strange symbols and the name, Issabella, manifested on Abby's mirror

I didn't know what to make of these symbols and words. Was Abby going into a trance because she was being possessed?

Who was Issabella? Was it a demonic force, or was it a spirit who needed help?

Abby and I continued to talk on a regular basis, and she would call me frequently with updates whenever a paranormal event took place at her home. I was trying my best to continue offering her guidance all the while, using prayers for her protection.

I was gravely concerned about the situation, even more so since Abby was pregnant. One night, she called and told me that she had gone into a trance, and when she came out, there was an upside-down cross carved onto her pregnant belly. It had been done with a screwdriver. She sent me an image of the mark, and I was shocked and disturbed by the event.

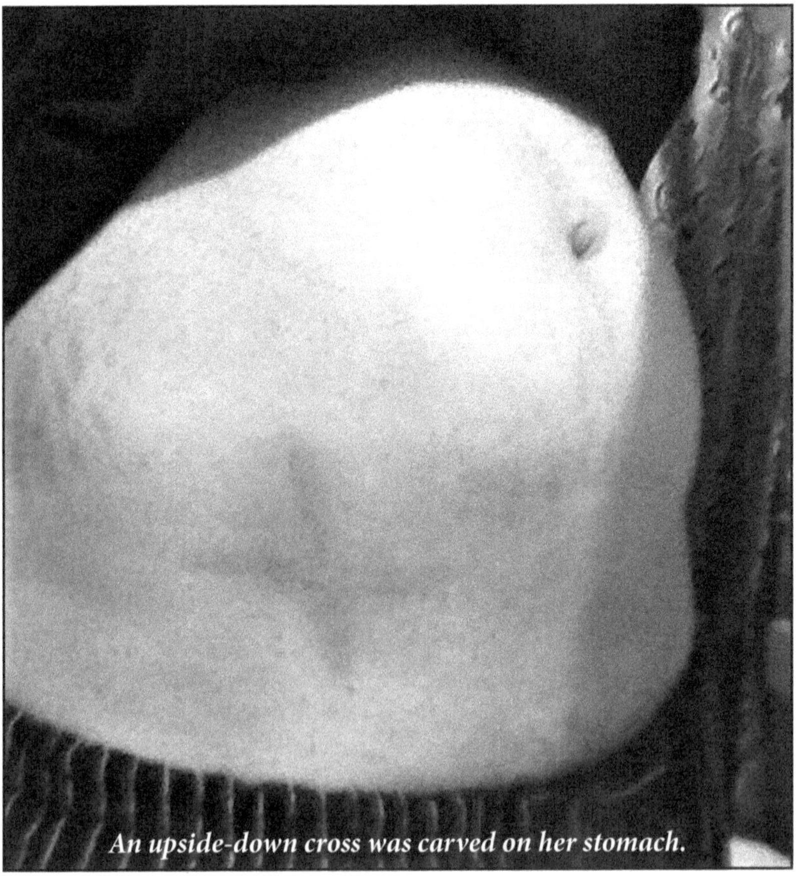

An upside-down cross was carved on her stomach.

This was an intense moment for me. Bear in mind, I was still getting a firm grasp of paranormal investigating and dealing with "the work" as it is called. In other words, I was still really delving into what it meant to be a demonologist. Here I was, looking at an image that could easily be out of a horror movie, but this was real. This was happening to an innocent girl, and she needed help. The reality of it all started to hit me on a different level at that time. To be honest, I felt like I was in over my head. I'd never dealt with, what could be, a legitimate possession. Now, here was a woman who was in big trouble and could well be possessed. Not only was she in danger, but even more disturbing, there was an unborn child to consider.

Flashes of Rosemary's Baby came into my head, and I thought this has got to be the absolute worse combination of things happening on a paranormal level. Still thinking about demons, satanic cults, and possessions, I reached out to demonologist John Zaffis, the nephew of Ed Warren. I had become acquainted with John and hoped that he would give me some input so I could help this poor girl get better.

John responded via email and told me, "You know Sean, these girls, they mess around with witchcraft, end up pregnant, then they have either complications with the baby, or the baby ends up dying."

I'm not sure exactly what I was hoping for, but this wasn't what I wanted to hear. I knew the situation was a heavy one, and it was becoming obvious to me that I would need to do all I could, myself, to help this girl. Most other paranormal investigators wouldn't go near it with a ten-foot pole, mostly because an unborn child was involved.

I started learning all I could about possession cases. These cases are difficult for a number of reasons. It's always hard to look at all the factors in a balanced way because so many lines get crossed. Faith is certainly a big factor, but it's important to look at the psychological components. In some cases, people's mental conditions can have a lot to do with the things that are manifesting. There are so many delicate aspects to confirming a real, legitimate possession of a human being.

After eliminating all the rational explanations, the next step is to move beyond and start looking at supernatural matters. The most important aspect is always to get help for the person, whether that is medical, psychological, or spiritual help, and that's where the trick is. That is what needs to be determined by an investigator. Getting the person safe and out of danger is, of course, the immediate priority.

This was a tough situation for me. I felt obligated to help Abby, and I wanted to, but I was also aware that I felt emotionally involved, thinking about her and her unborn child. This made the entire situation even more challenging, and I knew I needed to try my best to stay objective. I decided to dig deeper and see if I could learn more from Abby about her time dabbling in witchcraft, why she had gotten involved with it, and what she had been doing exactly. She started telling me some of the stories:

"When I was growing up, I went through a lot of things that were terrible. I had always been bullied and picked on in school. I was the average, normal, awkward teen—pimples, glasses, braces, etc. When I was fifteen years old, my great aunt always talked about the cult and witchcraft. She was in a coven. She told me some spells that could make me beautiful and popular, everything I wanted! She told me some of the books to use and certain spells to chant.

"I was curious and didn't think it was really real, so I was like, eh, what's the worst thing that could happen? So, I drew a pentagram with chalk on my floor, put a candle at each point, and one black one in the middle. I said the chant calling out to demons, cut my hand, and dripped blood into the black candle's flame. It shot up really high! I then felt whatever it was come into me. Things were never really right after that. Stuff had settled down for a while, but things started happening again when I got pregnant with my second child.

"My first child was three when things really spiked and started happening towards him. He met some sort of imaginary friend he called Nine. Nine would appear as a child around his age, maybe a little older. I knew kids had friends from time to time that were not really visible to others. My boy also did not have any complaints about Nine, nor was he scared of Nine. Not until one day when my child was playing in his playroom, and Nine was in there. I was in the kitchen cleaning, and I heard my child saying, 'Stop, you're scaring me! I don't want to play with you anymore.' Then the door shut.

"I quickly went to the door of his room and tried to open it, but it would not open. It was like it was locked. The crazy thing is, we don't have doorknobs that lock. I knew my three-year-old wasn't strong enough to hold the door shut! I finally got the door open after going completely mad, filled with panic, and saw my child was across the room in the middle of his toys, crying.

"I knew, then, that this thing, or spirit, Nine wasn't so friendly. Nine would get my child to do terrible things like try to drink a whole bottle of kid's Tylenol or stick a bobby pin in a light socket because 'it would be fun,' and this way, 'we could play with each other.'

"This Nine would say he was some little boy who had died nearby on the train tracks, but I was really starting to be concerned about what was truly going on and what was trying to influence my kid."

Obviously, this was an entirely different aspect of the case, and it was clear to me that the dark influences and entities involved had been around for a long time. Not only that, but it now seemed even more obvious that the starting point was Abby's involvement in witchcraft.

If this force around her had the power to do such physical things, what else had it already done, and what was to come? Abby told me about another weird incident, this one occurred when she was at a Pentecostal church.

There was a special guest at the church that day, a prophecy speaker. This man started calling out to the crowd, and out of nowhere, he pointed at Abby, picking her out of the throng of people. He said God was speaking to him and that he had an important message for her. Abby was a bit embarrassed at the time, not knowing what the man would say. He looked at her and pronounced:

"You have a darkness around you, young woman, and it follows you wherever you go. It is the path you went down that led you there, and God wants you to change what you acted out on in the past. The life choices are of Satan, and if you don't take God into your life, the darkness will take you over! You need to change and leave the path you came from. Be a true child of God." The speaker then touched Abby and started speaking in tongues. Of course, she had no clue what he was saying. Everyone's eyes were on her, making the situation all the more troubling.

I know Abby had a very difficult time growing up, and she endured a lot. The impressionable years are critical in how we develop as we age, and at such a time, we can be susceptible and vulnerable to a wide range of influences. Mistakes we make may be innocent but can also lead to dark events and situations. Demonic entities thrive on preying on the weak and vulnerable. They love to manipulate people and situations whenever they get the opportunity.

Sadly, Abby had all the traits of a classic victim of dark forces. A vulnerable girl who just wanted to be liked and have some success. Then along came an older person presenting a magical answer . . . it was a deadly cocktail of influences.

The situation with the entity, Nine, was another example of how, once these things have a victim in their sights, they don't let go, and they press for every opening they can find, even if it's an innocent child. In fact, they love to corrupt and damage innocents because it feeds their dark natures all the more.

This all made me think deeply about the nature of demons and the things they do. As the enemy of man, this is exactly the type of situation they thrive on. Remember, we're talking about a species at war with our kind on the physical plane and at war with God and his angels on the spiritual plane. The very reason for their putrid, evil nature and existence is because of the creation of mankind.

While Abby was going through her dark period in high school, she reached out to her aunt, who provided a path to salvation, at least, in a troubled teenage girl's eyes. These magic books seemed to be an answer, and she believed that witchcraft would give her everything she desired. But ultimately, it was all an illusion, and it opened the door for negative entities to enter her life.

It's typical of these kinds of situations. People get involved with witchcraft and other occult practices because they are looking for some kind of material gain or earthly benefit, hoping they can magically get anything they want. It always ends up being a twisted, dark path that leads to the witches getting some nasty things served up to them spiritually, emotionally, psychologically, and even physically. This was clearly the case with Abby, and the situation was very complicated. I continued to talk with Abby and delved further into her background in occult practices.

I learned more about some of the books Abby had utilized and found out that they provided her with detailed instructions for various black magic spells and rituals, as well as ways to communicate with various entities. The books were rich in dark incantations and methods of opening doorways to communing with evil entities. These methods of opening up such lines of contact were very dangerous. While Abby was hoping to communicate with spirits that would fulfill her desires, the entities that she was getting in touch with had their own agendas, none of them good.

There was this young girl, hoping for an end to her tortured loneliness, and here were these dark texts, telling her that all she had to do was call out to an unseen being and spill some of her own blood to get a quick solution.

I was disturbed, thinking about the whole thing. I've encountered a lot of these types of ritual experiences over the years, people getting involved with witchcraft, satanism, voodoo, all thinking that it was a simple thing and not realizing how spiritually dangerous these rituals and practices could become.

Saying those words, cutting herself, and spilling her blood on that black candle had set Abby on a very dark path, one that had haunted and tormented her for years, and things were getting worse all the time. She had made a contract with a dark entity, and it was going to collect one way or another.

Really, I didn't consider this all her fault, not at all. She had been the victim of bullies in school, and that is no laughing matter. Kids and teenagers can be absolutely horrible to each other and relentless in how they torment others who are not considered "cool." Combined with the other influences, Abby was a victim on many levels in this mess. No doubt, the idea of being able to tap into some kind of magic in order to get revenge on her tormentors had a great appeal to this young teenage girl. Ironically, sometime after she had started to dabble in the occult, some of Abby's bullies were in a very bad accident. She had to wonder, was she responsible? Had her rituals actually produced results?

As I pieced things together about Abby's situation, I learned that not only had her aunt given her spell books, but she had given her something else, too—an old, creepy doll. As it turned out, the doll's name was Issabella.

Issabella was the same name that had appeared written on a mirror, the name of a doll. This was beyond creepy. Why was the doll's name being written on the mirror? Was the doll possessed?

Considering that Abby's aunt had been well-versed in witchcraft, I had to wonder if Abby's aunt had done something to enchant the doll. Had she drawn some entity into the thing?

As I spoke to Abby more and more each week, I started to experience things myself. I can't express how unsettling this was on all fronts. On the one hand, it was a dark confirmation of the reality Abby was dealing with. On the other hand, it was disturbing that whatever was going on with this situation, whatever force was involved and attacking this woman, was now well-aware of my actions and my involvement in trying to help her.

Abby continued to call me with updates, and things continued to escalate. Around this time, she was living with her husband and her first child. Abby did a Skype call with me and showed me the creepy doll. I got a strange feeling looking at

Issabella, the doll

the thing and felt like it was glaring at me through the screen. Later that night when I was asleep, I had a clear vision of that doll. It was sitting up against a wall, but its head was turned away from me. As I watched, the doll's head suddenly turned, and the thing was staring straight at me, looking into my eyes.

I jumped awake with cold chills running over me. It was around three o'clock in the morning, and I had a hard time getting back to sleep after such a creepy experience. It was hard to get the image of that damn doll out of my head. After this, Abby told me that the doll was moving around her house. She said Issabella would show up in different rooms, even though no one in the house had moved her. Abby also told me that her aunt had many dolls. When Abby was a child, she always thought Issabella had a weird vibe, and it didn't sit right with her. Abby wondered why her aunt had given her the doll, but she didn't want to be rude and refuse a gift, so she accepted the creepy old thing.

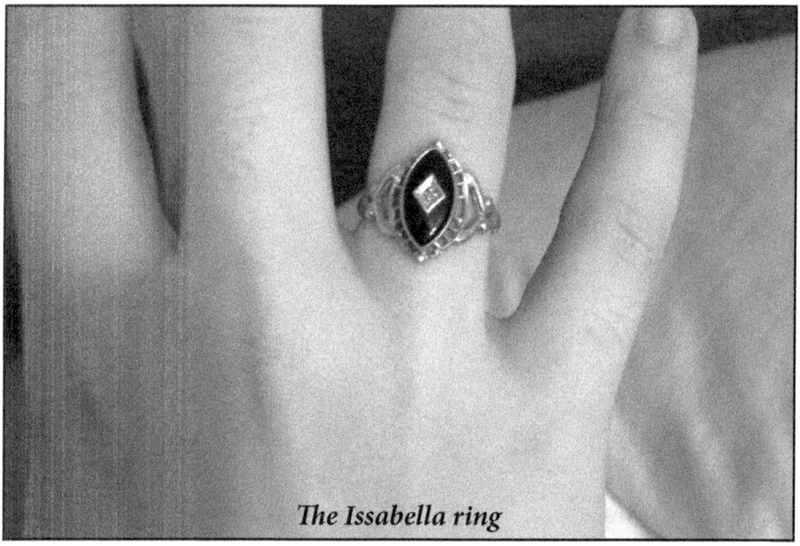

The Issabella ring

One day Abby walked into a room and saw Issabella there. The back of the doll was open, and Abby realized there was something inside of the doll. She pulled the item out and discovered it was a ring. It was black and gold in color. Abby had never seen the ring before and had no idea why it was in the doll. For whatever reason, she felt drawn to the ring and decided to put it on. After she did, she had second thoughts and decided to take the ring back off. It was stuck. Try as she might, Abby could not remove the ring. For three days, she tried every solution she could think of to loosen and remove the ring, but nothing worked. To top it off, the trances Abby was experiencing increased.

One night, while Abby was texting with me, she started to slip into a trance. Out of nowhere, I got an image of Abby standing in front of her bed. There in the background, was the creepy doll, Issabella, staring at the camera. It was perfectly in the middle of the bed and staring forward. Abby was dressed in some sort of old dress and was staring down. Her eyes were dilated. Why had she sent this to me?

I asked her, via text, what was wrong, asking what the picture was all about. It was a while before she responded, and she said that she couldn't recall anything that had happened, nor did she remember sending me the image.

More and more often, when I spoke with her, she would start to slip into one of those trances. I would be on the phone with her; she was talking normally, then suddenly she'd say she felt like she was going into a trance. There would be low whispers coming through the speaker on my phone. I couldn't understand what she was saying, and it was definitely some other sort of language, not anything I'd heard before.

I started to record audio of the conversations to capture the voice that she was speaking. I plugged some of this audio into my computer and listened to it with headphones, trying hard to distinguish what was being said, looking for clues to what language was being spoken. It was very difficult to understand, though part of it, at least, sounded like Latin. I kept experimenting with the audio. Finally, I tried playing the track in reverse. I was in complete shock and unsettled to my core when I realized the track was indeed English—spoken in reverse!

Once again, my mind raced thinking about the situation's

intensity, and I thought about how much it was like something out of a demonic possession movie. It seemed that with each new series of events, I, personally, hit a new level of realization about the serious nature of this case. But despite the continued feeling that I was in over my head, I could not stop. I was too committed at this point and genuinely wanted to help this girl anyway I could.

For me, this was another important stage in my personal journey, and in many ways, one of my biggest challenges. I knew that I needed to continue to do all I could and document every aspect of the situation. Ghosts and hauntings are one thing, but a situation involving something clearly demonic was on a vastly different level and much, much more serious.

As the weeks went on, I continued to talk to Abby getting updates and additional information with each conversation. I was more and more invested, and I would often experience various levels of anxiety and other feelings related to what she was going through. These feelings made it more difficult for me to stay detached and objective, but what was I going to do? Adding to the difficulties, this girl really had no one else to talk to, so I was the primary person hearing about these experiences and trying to help her. Her calls were often frantic cries for help, and I continued to do my best as the activity levels continued to build week after week.

One evening Abby called me on the verge of tears. The level of her fear was so intense it seemed to radiate through the phone. In the background, I could hear her child screaming, all because Abby, the mom, was freaking out. Abby told me she felt like she was about to pass out, and I felt helpless being at such a distance. These types of calls were all too frequent, and even though I could document the incidents, I still wasn't sure exactly what to do in practical, physical terms.

I always tried to run a recorder when Abby called. She would go silent, and I would sit there waiting while the recorder was running. Strange, fast whispers would come through the phone. Again, it sounded like someone speaking something similar to Latin, at least in bits and pieces. I wondered if somehow, something was actually speaking reverse English as

I had discovered on the earlier recording. If this was the case, how was it even possible? What exactly was coming through this woman?

One night, Abby called, telling me she couldn't breathe and felt something taking her over. I heard, very clearly, laughter coming over the phone. It was dark and malicious, and I immediately started reciting the St. Michael prayer to see if it would help. I touched my St. Michael pendant as I said the prayer. My pendant was touched by a true relic of the cross, so it has both personal associations as well as added spiritual power for me. It never leaves its place around my neck.

While Abby felt like she was being choked, I continued the prayer of protection. Just then, I started to feel a burning sensation on my right arm. I looked down and was shocked to find marks on my arm. It looked as if I had been scratched or slashed with something. I looked carefully and counted thirteen separate slash marks. Amid all of this, voices were coming from over the phone, manifesting around Abby. I could hear something say, "There's a demon inside you," and "Hail Beezlebub." These muttering demonic voices seemed to come from Abby part of the time. On other occasions, they seemed to manifest from her three-year-old son.

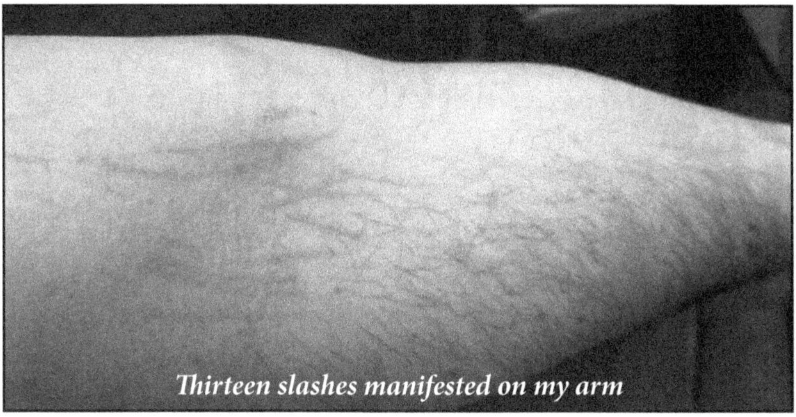

Thirteen slashes manifested on my arm

These events made things much, much more disturbing, especially the references to Beelzebub. During the course of my studies in becoming a demonologist, I had learned a lot about this particular demon and his many associations with darkness. Beelzebub is a prince of demons. His name is a distortion of Baal-Zebul, the chief Canaanite or Phoenician god. Originally meaning "Lord of the Divine Abode" or "Lord of the Heavens," his distorted name means "Lord of the Flies." He is said to manifest as a gigantic, gruesome-looking fly or as something monstrous in size sitting on a throne. Some images show him with a swollen face and chest, large nostrils, horns, bat wings, a lion's tail, feet like a duck, and a covering of thick, black matted hair. He was worshiped in ancient times and later recognized as a major demon by some Abrahamic religions.

This demon is mentioned in the New Testament. He is referenced in the book of Matthew after the scribes accuse Jesus of using the demon's power to drive out other demons. Jesus, himself, clarifies their mistaken assumption:

"Jesus knew their thoughts and said to them, 'Every kingdom divided against itself will be ruined, and every city or household divided against itself will not stand. If Satan drives out Satan, he is divided against himself. How then can this kingdom stand? And if I drive out demons by Beelzebul, by whom do your people drive them out? So then, they will be your judges. But if I drive out demons by the Spirit of God, then the kingdom of God has come upon you'" (Matthew 12: 25-28).

Early accounts depict Beelzebub as a fearsome and feared demon. He identifies himself as the "ruler of all demons." Whether this can be considered accurate or not is up to debate since technically, Lucifer would be the ruler of all demons. Some theological sources actually indicate that Beelzebub is just another name for Satan himself. Though, this is contradicted by later writings.

Some stories say that after the crucifixion of Jesus, Satan bragged to Beelzebub that he would take Jesus to hell in revenge for having been defeated so many times by him. Beelzebub argued that this was a bad idea since Jesus was too powerful, and his presence would upset the balance of hell. When Jesus arrived, Beelzebub pushed Satan away from the mouth of hell and barricaded the gate against Jesus, calling out to other demons to help, but they could not keep Jesus out. Jesus trampled over Satan and broke the chains of souls imprisoned in hell, releasing trapped saints who immediately ascended to heaven.

All of this was fascinating information, and over the years, I have noticed that this entity has shown up frequently in paranormal cases. But there was one aspect of this demon that had a special relationship to Abby and the horrible things she was going through: Beelzebub is strongly associated with witches.

During medieval times, this connection became commonly recognized. Beelzebub was said to reign over witches' Sabbats. In some texts, it is stated that he was a demon of great power and one that witches prayed to along with Satan.

Medieval texts also said that witches denied the power of Christ and chanted the name of Beelzebub as they danced in ritual. The unholy eucharist bread that witches used had the image of this demon imprinted on it.

There are tales of Beelzebub mating with witches during wild orgies and demonic ceremonies. It was said that witches would gather together around a dark altar and lay flat on the ground in a semicircle. They would swallow a foul potion that caused them to sweat and become frozen in place. While lying there in this bizarre state, the demon Beelzebub would appear among them, and a frenzied orgy would begin as he copulated with each one in turn.

Stories of this demon continued into the 17th century when "Black Masses" became a fashionable trend among members of high society who were looking for something daring to try. Magical grimories mentioned this hideous demon and some even cautioned against contacting him, writing that to do so was to risk various afflictions as well as death. Once conjured, the demon is very difficult to banish.

There couldn't be a coincidence between the fact that Abby's troubles had started with her exploration of witchcraft and that this particular demon was now manifesting around her. Not only was he strongly associated with witches, but his name had also turned up during some famous possession cases, notably, the reported possessions in Laon, France in 1566 and the bewitchment of nuns in the Loudun possession case at the Ursuline convent in 1634 in France.

It was absolutely chilling to realize that here was a woman who had delved into witchcraft and was now suffering what appeared to be possession to some degree, and now a demon was making itself known, the very one often associated with both witchcraft and possession. It was a sickening feeling, and I felt chills all over my body, realizing the depth of what was happening and what I was in the middle of.

I continued to use a recorder to capture the weird language that was manifesting during conversations with Abby. The language still sounded like a form of Latin, but often had hints of English and Spanish. As I had discovered earlier, playing the recordings backward revealed words that could be understood. I utilized a software that enabled me to reverse the recording and listen to it to determine what these entities were saying. Sentences began to emerge from the strange audio tracks.

"It's an exorcism."

"He saw the baby in a dream."

"She needs an exorcism, and they know."

It was yet another level of creepiness added to what I had already been experiencing. Here was more confirmation of the demonic element and the storm that I was in the midst of. This thing's presence and its awareness of me soon became even more obvious. Abby called one night in one of her frenzied states. I asked her what was going on, and she told me that "it" was trying to take her over again. She went silent, and I knew what was going to happen next, she was going to slip into one of her trance states and perhaps start talking in the strange language again.

I waited a few moments and heard a low-toned male voice come over the phone's speaker. Right away, I started to pray the rosary. Hail Mary, full of grace . . . I repeated it over and over, doing my best to stay focused on the power of my faith, all while waiting to see what would happen with Abby. As I continued saying my prayers, the thing decided to address me.

"Seannn, she's mine," a demonic voice stated.

The voice chilled me to the bone. It wasn't Abby's voice at all, and it didn't even sound like anything human. It was as if there were three voices all layered together, all speaking in unison. I was silent for a moment, as the gravity of this manifestation sunk in. As I was trying to fully wrap my head around this, the voice repeated, "Seannn, she's mine."

This time I responded to the thing and stated, "No, she's a child of the Lord." Regaining my focus, I started repeating my prayers again, focusing on Abby's soul and spirit and trying to lend her spiritual strength to push the influence off of her. After a few moments of this, I heard coughing on the other end of the phone and a moaning sound. I stopped and asked, "Abby, are you okay?"

She sounded like she had just woken up and like she was crying with sadness. Unfortunately, this wouldn't be the last time I would speak to the evil presence attempting to control this girl.

While the primary focus had been on Abby and her unborn child, there was another individual who was being deeply affected by the sinister things occurring around this young woman—her three-year-old son.

I can only imagine what was going on in this little boy's mind as he tried to understand and comprehend the things happening to his mother and the strange things that he, himself, was seeing and hearing.

Dark forces love to manipulate and spiritually harm children, and this demonic presence was doing whatever it could to torture the boy. The boy would say disturbing things to his mother. He would speak the name Beelzebub, not a name that a three-year-old should know! He would also talk about Issabella, the creepy doll that Abby had.

Even darker, it was clear that the demon had been manifesting to the little boy for some time. At first, he appeared to the child in the form of another little boy, one in spirit form, and became the invisible friend known as Nine.

Nine, in his guise as another little boy, told Abby's son that he had died on a set of train tracks nearby. He tried to convince Abby's son to do things that would lead to the boy dying, himself, so they could be together.

But there were other things, too. The spirit would tell the boy to go to the door of his room and turn the handle nine times. It's not always clear or easy to understand why demonic forces do things like instructing someone to do something a certain number of times.

I thought about this incident and wondered if this was another way for the dark entities to mock the Holy Trinity. I recalled that there are nine choirs of holy angels, as well as nine choirs of hell, so there could be some connection there.

Of course, it's also notable that this was the same door that had slammed shut and that Abby could not get open with all her strength. Had the demon done some kind of enchantment on the door?

On another occasion, Abby called me in the evening and said her son was acting very strangely. He kept going on and on about what he called "the big bad wolf." Now, of course, this would maybe not be a concern if the boy was talking about fairy tales or stories, but there was a very sinister edge to his version of the wolf—he told his mother that the one he saw had the "mark of the beast 666." In fact, I could hear the boy in the background as Abby told me what was going on. He was sort of singing about it, "The big bad wolf, the big bad wolf . . . he has the mark of the beast 666."

This was so disturbing; I felt the blood drain out of my face and had that sickening feeling wash over me. The depths to which this thing would go, and how it would interfere with this family, were so terrible.

Hearing what was going on in real-time, I decided to try a test. I recalled reading a piece by a priest who pointed out that a possessed person, or someone under demonic influence, would be unable to say the phrase, "I love Jesus." I told Abby to ask her son to say something else, "Ask him to say, I love Jesus," I told her. I listened as she made the request of her son. Immediately, the kid began howling in the background. Once he started, he would not stop. He kept on and on. After a moment, he told his mother that he wanted the phone. She gave it to him, and I heard this kid on the other end say to me, "You better watch out tonight. The big, bad wolf, he bites. He will bite your penis off and spit it on your chest."

I had no words. This was coming from the mouth of a three-year-old boy. There is no way this young child could have come up with such a foul phrase as an instant response to my request, asking him to state that he loved Jesus.

I thought about this incident for a long time, and it was on my mind that night when I turned in for bed. I knew that I would need to be even more on guard as I continued to move forward, helping Abby. That night, I woke up to a weird pinching feeling on my arm. I turned on the light and looked at the spot. There was, what looked like, a bite mark on my arm. Was this thing making its presence known in a very physical way? Considering what the kid had said to me, I was thankful that the bite appeared on my arm and not elsewhere!

A few days later, I received an afternoon call from Abby. At least, it was her number, but when I picked up the phone, all I could hear was screaming. It turned out to be Abby's friend, Janet, on the other end. I listened to the screams and other noises—banging and pelting sounds like something hitting metal. It became obvious that both Abby and her friend were screaming. Janet was on the phone because Abby was driving. It was difficult to even get a word out of them, which made it hard to determine exactly what was happening.

Finally, Janet was able to tell me that blackbirds were slamming into the vehicle, loads and loads of them were striking it, which explained the odd pelting sound I was hearing. The girls finally pulled over and stopped the car. I'm not sure why they didn't do this sooner, maybe because of the situation's weirdness and the shock of what was happening. Either way, once they pulled over, the bird attacks stopped. I could hear the two women over the phone. Both of them were breathing heavily, clearly still somewhat panicked. Janet was yelling at Abby, asking her what the hell was going on and what this was all about.

Later that night, Abby called to tell me there was a scratching sound on the wall and a strong sulfur smell in the room that emanated from nowhere. She had some friends over at her house during this time, which presented other difficulties. How do you explain such things to people? But it got stranger. She set the phone down, and I could hear some of the friends asking her what she was doing. One of them picked up the phone and told me that Abby had a weird look in her eyes. As they watched her, she suddenly ran into the laundry room. They followed her and saw her jump on top of the washing machine, get on all fours, and look at them with what they called a "dark smile."

They thought maybe Abby was just joking around, and after a few minutes, she climbed down off the washer and returned to normal. She would later tell me that these kinds of things were happening even when others weren't present. She would be in one place in the house, and the next thing she knew, she was somewhere else, snapping out of whatever had happened.

Abby also said that she would suddenly find herself out on the front lawn from time to time. One night she went to bed, fell asleep, then came to with her hands covered with dirt. She was using her nails, digging in the dirt in the yard. She had no clue what she was digging for. This happened several times, and she could never determine what it was all about.

Other things were happening in the house too. Abby would constantly have the feeling that someone or something was watching her. She would take pictures with her phone and send them to me on many occasions. Often, there would be weird images in the photos. At one point, I saw what looked like a witch's face in the hallway. On another occasion, something with red eyes was staring at her through her window.

She was getting constantly scratched. At one point, she took a video, and scratches could be seen, forming on her with nothing there to explain the manifestation. Even her son was having scratches manifest on him, usually in threes, again, a mocking of the Holy Trinity.

I felt terrible about the situation. I could only imagine what Abby was going through as she helplessly watched something unseen harm her son. Other than trying to calm the boy, there was little she could do but hope for an end to the supernatural torment.

Of course, it was very disturbing to hear about the scratches that would form on her pregnant belly. She sent an image of one of them to me, what appeared to be a circle with a line going through it. Something about it rang a bell, and I remembered the weird writing that had shown up earlier on her mirror. Double-checking this, I confirmed that it was indeed the same symbol.

I checked with an occult specialist about the symbol. He didn't recognize it at first, and it took some digging, but he finally learned that it was an old symbol that had some kind of association with fertility. I was disturbed by the news. Did this thing want Abby's baby? My mind raced, and my emotions were all over the place. She soon called me again, another frantic call, another horrific experience unfolding. This time I was driving, so I wasn't prepared to record the conversation.

I heard dark laughter come through over our conversation. Abby was gasping for air. Something was choking her again, and I started to pray out loud. The line went silent. I heard her son in the background, and he picked up the phone. I was able to determine that his mother was unresponsive. Before I could make another move, the boy said, "Whoa, look at Mommy. She's floating."

I almost dropped the phone and quickly blurted out, "Are you kidding me?" The boy responded by saying, again, that his mother was floating in the air.

The only thing I could think of was to try to get this little boy to take a video or a picture of what was happening. I knew he was only a three-year-old little boy, but I had to know If there was any possibility of getting a picture, I had to see this. Was this girl really levitating? And if so, what was causing it?

Once the incident was over, and Abby came on the line, I asked her if she was okay. She confirmed she was and didn't seem to have much idea about what had happened or why. This was typical, of course. Sadly, I hadn't had any luck getting Abby's son to take a video of the levitating incident, but the whole thing led me to think about another different approach that could be used in the case.

When I next talked to Abby, I told her that she needed to try to capture some of the weird events on video, if at all possible. I told her that the next time she felt like she was going into a trance, she should set her phone on video record and place it somewhere it would, hopefully, catch whatever was happening to her and what she was doing.

Using this method, it wasn't long before she captured something on video. I still have the footage and still find it disturbing. In the beginning, there was a low-guttural growl and a man's voice yelling out, "It's Beelzebub!" Abby started to convulse forward, and it looked like she was getting choked as she loudly gasped for air. Her son was next to her, and he started climbing over her as this was happening. He can be heard in the video saying, "Mommy, wake up . . . Please, Mommy, wake up," as he attempted to shake her out of the trance. After a couple of minutes, she did come out of the trance, in tears, but finally able to breathe.

Sometimes the demonic entity would interfere with calls or videos. One night, as we spoke on Skype, the screen started to glitch, and Abby's face looked like it was changing. I took a screenshot of this, and the call immediately went dead.

I looked closely at the image I had taken of the call. There were some odd things about the picture. First, it looked as if someone else's eyes were over Abby's face during the glitch. Not only that, but over her left shoulder, there was a dark shadow. I looked at it closely and saw that it was the side profile of a face with red eyes!

Here it was—an image of the thing responsible for the activity around this girl and her family. For me, this was crystal clear evidence of the demonic presence in their home. Every time my phone rang, and I saw Abby's number pop up, I took a deep breath, wondering what next? What kind of manifestation

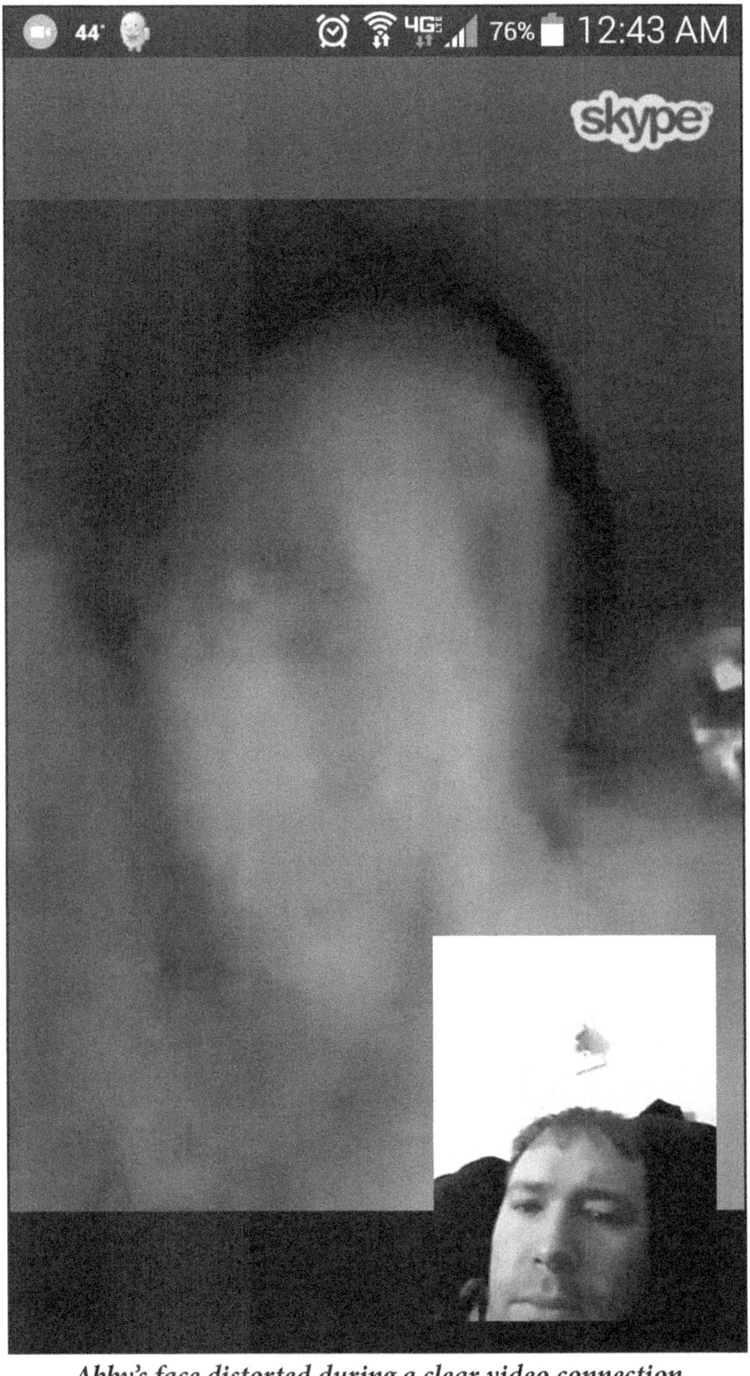

Abby's face distorted during a clear video connection

was taking place, and what type of attack was underway?

I always did my best to be a calming influence to keep her focused and centered on God's power and the forces of good. I was challenged, myself, during the course of this, and could only imagine what she was going through on emotional and mental levels. Whenever possible, I would always grab my recorder, letting it run during the course of our conversations, whether we were talking or whether there was complete silence. I knew full well that this thing, this foul demonic presence, was well-aware of me and what I was doing to help this girl. During one point of silence, when I felt the thing was there on the other end, I asked, "Are you using Abby's body as a vessel?"

"Nooo," It replied.

"Were you ever alive?" I asked it.

"NEVER!" came the loud response.

I decided, at the moment, to try another test. I didn't say a word but grabbed a small crucifix that I keep in my bedroom. It's about six inches long, and I took it in my hand, putting it right up to the phone while the demon was there. The moment I did this, there was a loud, hissing sound that came through the phone. I tell you, there wasn't a place on my body that didn't feel the chills at that moment. I was defending my faith on a whole new level, at least for myself.

The thing on the other end of the phone screamed at me. Again, it was a chilling moment, and I immediately started praying, calling on the power of God and St. Michael. A loud growl came from the other end of the line, and once again, I heard screams, this time, they were layered as if multiple . . . I didn't know what things . . . were screaming. It was unholy and unearthly.

As the screams continued, so did my prayers. I wasn't about to let this thing stop me. After a few moments, the horrible screams stopped, and the sound of Abby coughing came. I knew she was free, at least for the moment. Her voice returned, along with the fear of what had just happened and the reminder that this thing could still take her and control parts of her life.

The weeks went on, and there were constant calls, continued states of trance and panic, and more photos of strange manifestations in her home. She sent a picture to me that showed two bar stools, turned so that their legs were facing each other, but weirdly twisted together in a way that seemed impossible. She kept hearing scratching sounds in her walls, and the sickening sulfur smell would continue to manifest in her home.

Sometimes she would call, choking and gasping for air. There would be demonic laughing over the sounds of her voice as if something was being completely entertained by her struggles. The strange voices continued to speak in the mixed tongue of Latin and backward English.

While I did all I could to help, there were logistic challenges with the situation. I was living in New York while Abby was in the deep south. I simply couldn't rush over to her house when these incidents happened. Work and other concerns made it more difficult to get there to help her in person, and honestly, I wasn't completely sure what more I could do in person. But there was something that I had been working on that I did believe would make a difference—I wanted to get a priest to go to her house.

This may sound like a simple thing, but really it wasn't, not at all. First, it's important to understand that Abby was in the rural south. There weren't many priests in close range who could visit her where she was living. Beyond that, there are not many priests who even want to address such matters. They would rather just have people come to church each weekend and receive their communion and blessings there. I frequently prodded Abby about this, and she did reach out in her region, trying to find someone to, at least come, and bless the home.

Finally, she was able to get a priest who agreed to come to the home. He showed up and proceeded to set up to do the blessing. Abby's son saw the man and wasn't happy. The boy told him, "We don't want you here. You can leave."

The priest looked at the boy and said, "I'm here to help you, young man."

The boy clearly wasn't happy about the situation but didn't respond. As the priest started to do the blessing, he started to feel somewhat off and became nauseous. Abby hadn't told the man what had been transpiring in the house or to her. She was too worried about judgment and afraid that he wouldn't come to do the blessing.

The priest finished the blessing and left. There's no telling what he thought, personally, or what he was picking up on while doing his spiritual work. The house blessing did at least give some temporary relief, but it certainly wasn't a cure, and it wasn't long before the activity was going full speed again.

One night, after one of her trance experiences, Abby described the entity that she had seen, "He had long, pointed ears with bells on the end and bright, white eyes with small black lashes. He had three sets of sharp-looking teeth, and he was brown, looking almost like a lizard, and he was built with sheep-like legs with grey feathers on them. His nose was just two holes like slashes."

What a creepy image this conjured! She drew a picture of the thing and sent it to me. Because of my connection to the case and her description of the thing, I had an even clearer picture of it. Not only that, but this entity showed up in a vision that I'd had. It was definitely the same creature, but its features were kind of blurry when I saw it. In my vision, it was lurking in the dark.

I had other visions associated with Abby, and whatever was after her. One night I had a vision that I was in a room, and Abby was there, leaning up against a wall. I was looking at her face and could see both of her eyes. They were changing color, going through multiple colors of light as if there was a prism of some kind in her eyes. She had a spaced-out expression, and I knew that she was slipping into one of her trance states. As I was watching this, I sensed a presence next to me. I didn't turn to look at it, but I knew it was there. I suddenly felt sharp teeth biting down on my ear lobe. I felt a piercing pain from the bite. Then, there was a long, drawn-out whisper in my ear. "Astarte," said a creepy, female voice in my ear.

Abby's drawing of the entity

I had never heard the word before, but over my years being involved in demonology, I've found that often words, names, or phrases will come to me telepathically or in a vision and prove relevant to a case. Of course, getting a word like this always leads me to delve into research to see what I can find and what connections I can make. In this case, it was back to the ancients again.

Initial research revealed that in ancient Phoenicia, Astarte was the great goddess of fertility, motherhood, and war. What a strange combination, I thought. Of course, the connections to the case were obvious to a degree. There had been mentions of fertility in Abby's case with the strange symbol that had shown up, and obviously, she was pregnant and already a mother. But it was odd that a mother goddess would also be a goddess of war, and I found the idea bothersome.

Delving into the research further, I learned that Astarte was the counterpart of the Babylonian goddess, Ishtar, and one of the oldest Middle Eastern representations of the goddess dating back to the Neolithic and Bronze Ages. The first recorded reference to Astarte actually dates back to 1478 B.C.E., but her cult was already well-established by then. Her followers spread westward from Phoenicia into ancient Greece, Rome, and as far as the British Isles.

She was portrayed by the Phoenicians with cow horns, a sign of fertility. She was also shown caressing a child in some images. Again, this was very disturbing information, considering the involvement of children and the depiction of a horned entity. Even more unsettling was the information I discovered about her origins. She was said to have descended to the earth as a fiery star, landing near Byblos in a lake at Alphaca.

I immediately thought about Lucifer and his fellow fallen angels who were cast out of heaven. Was there some connection between the two? It is interesting to note that her worship was condemned by the prophets of the Old Testament. Her followers were known to worship the goddess in wild sexual rituals, and sacrifices were made to her that included firstborn children and newborn animals.

I also learned that Astarte is associated with the moon, and in old pagan traditions, she was a "giver of life." She also supposedly rules the spirits of the dead. I was well-aware that often, the goddesses that witches worship are "moon goddesses," and the connection to witchcraft again sprang to mind. As is often the case, numerous threads of information were all coming together into a whole picture, one that was very complex and had ties to ancient rituals. God only knew the true intent of these entities and how far they were willing to push this woman. I also had to wonder how long this had been underway. Had Abby's aunt been guided by some unseen force to push the young girl into dark ceremonies that would open a door for these beings to return?

I continued to research, exploring the various connections and implications of the information. While I had heard Beelzebub quite a few times, this was a new demonic association that hadn't come up until now. How did it play a part in Abby's spiritual affliction?

As the weeks flew by, it was getting closer and closer to Abby's due date, and I was growing more and more concerned. I told her that when the baby was born, no matter what it took, she needed to find a way to have the child baptized as soon as possible. I wanted everything that could be done for the safety of the child to be done.

The day of the child's birth finally arrived. I can tell you; it was a stressful time, and there was lots of anxiety, not knowing what was going to happen. I was so delighted to find out that Abby was able to have a priest come and bless the baby. Her newborn took her first breath on her own in this world, and Abby sent photos to me as soon as she was able. For me, the most comforting moment was watching a video of the baby getting blessed with holy oil on her forehead and baptized at the hospital.

Sadly, the good feelings and comfort would be short-lived. The baby had complications with her lungs. Apparently, the child's lungs were not developed enough. The baby had to be hooked up to a machine and continuously monitored.

This was a terrible development. I sat there thinking about the child's situation, and my mind raced back to what John Zaffis had told me. Young women messing around with witchcraft often got pregnant, resulting in health complications and even death.

Abby, herself, didn't seem to be in danger health-wise at this point, but the child certainly was. A lot of people would say, "Oh, it's just a medical complication; these things happen, and you just need to let the doctors fix it." But given everything that had transpired, the demonic forces that were clearly in operation in Abby's life, and the power that they had already displayed, I had to wonder, what evil force was at work harming this innocent baby and what was its end game?

After a time, the baby was able to be at home with Abby, although the little one was still on a machine. Dark things continued to manifest in the home. Abby was still going into the bizarre trances. She would continually find herself outside on her hands and knees, digging away in the dirt with her hands.

The incidents became even more dangerous. At one point, she was taking a bath, trying to relax, when something suddenly pushed her head down under the water. She struggled to get her head back up for air, but whatever force was holding her was very strong. Somehow, the thought of leaving her children behind gave her enough energy to push up out of the water.

Abby's son continued to be a frequent focal point of activity in the home. One night, she heard the boy singing a song, "Draw the cross upside-down, draw the cross upside-down, draw the cross upside-down." Going into the playroom, Abby found him with his shirt off, singing away and making the motion of drawing an upside-down cross on his chest with his fingers.

Her son also continued having conversations with his invisible friend, Nine, though at times, the son was clearly resistant to what the entity was telling him to do. Her son would get angry and tell Nine that he didn't want to play with him anymore and didn't want to do mean or bad things. But the boy gave in or was coerced on some occasions.

One night, Abby was in the kitchen when she heard the alert going off on her baby's breathing machine. She rushed into the nursery to find her son there. He had pulled one of the plugs off from the baby's breathing machine! Abby screamed at him and rushed to fix the cord. "Why in the hell would you do such a thing?" She yelled at her son.

The response was chilling, "Beelzebub told me to do it."

Abby called me right away to tell me about the incident. She said her son had a strange look on his face and that he was hardly recognizable. "It's as if it isn't my son anymore," she told me.

The situation got even creepier when the little boy started talking to his mother in a sexual manner, telling her what he wanted to do to her. He even tried to jump on her and grab at her breast in a sexual manner.

Abby was able to get a picture of her son's face during his verbal display, and she sent it to me. I couldn't believe how the kid looked. His eyes were cast down with a weird stare that greatly disturbed me. This was the face of a young child controlled by something demonic. Thinking about the horror of the situation, I simply had no words.

Most of the activity continued in cycles. One minute, everything would be fine, then suddenly the baby would have a bad health scare, and things would kick up around the house, and the manifestations would continue, scratching in the walls, the smell of sulfur, and the violent choking attacks.

Abby's son kept talking about Nine and Beelzebub. Photos taken in the home would show bizarre figures, demon-like things, witch's faces, and more.

I still struggled to find answers, find more ways to help this woman and her children, keep them safe, and somehow free them from the demonic influences playing hell with their lives. Would this all end in tragedy, or would the family be able to find spiritual peace? Answers soon came.

One day, Abby was holding her newborn baby when something seemed amiss. The baby had a strange look about her.

Suddenly, there was a weird groaning sound from the child. The baby was staring off into nothing and started to change color. Abby thought the baby was choking and watched in horror as the little one turned blue. As soon as Abby realized something was wrong, she called in the emergency, and paramedics arrived soon after. They did all they could trying to save the baby, but it was too late. The child had passed away.

I can't imagine the horror, the sadness of losing a child. It seems like the worst tragedy imaginable. Doctors later determined that the child had had heart problems in addition to its lung issue. It had all been too much for the little one to survive.

I won't even try to express the depths of the personal nightmare that Abby was going through due to losing her child. On top of everything else that had occurred, it must have been unimaginable.

For me, the loss hit deeply. Although I was at a distance, I had become attached to this family, their lives, and trials. I understood now why no one else had been willing to jump in and try to help with this case. It was simply too fraught with potential tragedies like the one that had now occurred.

It felt like I had failed, yet I knew there was nothing else I could have done given the circumstances. Doctors were unable to see all the issues, and without a diagnosis, no one knew what other treatments the child might have needed or if they would have been enough. But beyond this, I sat and wondered, why had this girl been sent to me in the first place? It was one of those moments when even the most faithful question God, but I was just looking for answers. I do believe that things happen for a reason; that people meet for a reason. If we're called together or brought into someone's life, there's a purpose or a lesson behind it. It is our responsibility to find those secret meanings and determine what the connection means.

I was crushed at the news of the baby's passing and knew that it would take time before things became clearer about the events that had transpired.

I later thought about some of the possible meanings

connected to Abby and her family. After a conversation with her, I realized that the child had lived for eighteen months. My mind sprang to the Bible and the number. According to biblical symbology, the number represents bondage. In the book of Judges, it is recorded that the children of Israel were in bondage to several nations before Saul was made king. Specifically, it is written that, Eglon, the Moabite king, and the Philistines (with the help of the people of Ammon), oppressed the Israelites for eighteen years. The number turned up on other occasions, too. Jesus healed a woman who had a "spirit of infirmity" within her. The spirit had kept her "bent over" for eighteen years.

Maybe this was all a stretch, but maybe not. I always look for synchronicities in these cases, and so often, I find connections that give a greater overview of what is really operating below the surface. Demonic forces love to play these games, to hide clues in the use of numbers and other related bits and pieces. Thinking about it all, I realized another curious fact; there was a connection with the most well-known demonic number—666. Using numerology, 6+6+6=18.

And of course, Abby's son had been singing about the mark of the beast 666.

I couldn't ignore the connections. Something very dark was indeed manipulating things on some level. Perhaps just to poke at us, or maybe just to make it obvious that it had power and COULD manipulate things. Either way, it was unsettling and evil.

This brings us to the present. Of course, the burning question on everyone's minds at this point is, what happened to Abby after these events? Does she still experience paranormal and demonic activity? The short answer is no, not really. Once her baby passed away, the activity went dormant. There was something about the birth that brought things to an unholy culmination. We can only speculate why this is the case.

Abby and I are still in touch, and we speak on a regular basis. When I worked on my first book, I thought about including her story, but it was left alone due to the emotional intensity. It was uncertain if or how the account would ever be told. After all, the story is deeply personal and tragic. After speaking with Abby, we both agreed on the importance of the account. Ultimately, by sharing this story, maybe others will be helped. I can't express strongly enough the dangers of witchcraft and dark rituals. It's a path that leads to tragedy and misery. Abby's story should make that very clear. I say to anyone thinking of dabbling in such things, please, please don't. You won't just be risking your own spirit, but your family's as well. Ignore the malevolent forces that make promises and turn instead to God's light.

While I was writing this story, I was also investigating various haunted locations, and references to Abby's story would frequently come through various ghost boxes. Aside from her name, I would receive references to Nine, the witch, baby, pregnancy, and more, all unmistakably linked to the story.

You may wonder why this is the case. I believe it's because devils and demons don't really want the spotlight to shine on their activities. These things operate in darkness, and part of that darkness is people not believing how real they are. If more people realized, then more people would be on guard against such things. So, the very fact that I was documenting the story and had committed to having it in this book bothered the dark forces involved.

While I said that the activity around Abby had gone dormant, I should mention that although her family is not tormented by evil entities anymore, there are still occasional, small things that occur. I stayed up late one night, finishing my notes on Abby's story. The next morning, I received a message from her. She'd had a vivid dream and felt compelled to tell me about it:

"You were in my dream last night, Sean. You came to my house and told me you needed me to help you complete what was started and not finished.

"We go to these woods, and you tell me to grab your hands so we can channel it and to trust you. I did, but things got dark, and the ground shook. Then you shape-shifted into a female with a nightgown on. She looked like she had been buried for decades. She gave me a pendant and told me to complete the ritual so it would all be over. I then started chanting, and all the leaves came up from the ground and spun around me like I was controlling the wind. Then I lifted into the air, and when I drifted back down, I was in a graveyard, and you were there. It was like I was looking through the veil, and I was trying to tell you that the witch from the state I live in was coming. But all that came out was witch, ritual, and the name of the state over and over.

"You kept saying "weird," and "that's insane." I tried so hard to get to you for help, but chains came from the woods behind the graveyard and wrapped around my neck, wrists, and ankles and pulled me into the woods into a shallow grave. Then, as I was about to take my last breath from suffocation, I saw lights shining through, and I woke up."

It was strange that Abby had this dream the same night I was finishing her story. What was the connection, and what exactly did the dream mean? Perhaps it was symbolic of getting the story out, freeing herself from its secrets, but I couldn't be sure.

Aside from the dream experience, Abby has told me that on occasion, little things happen here and there, but they are very, very minor compared to the insane high state of activity that had once been constant in her home. She stays on guard and is always watchful in case the small sensations aren't just memories or residual energies, but something of a dark nature rearing its ugly self. I'm glad that she let me share this story and the recent dream she had connected to this intense time in her life. I asked her if there was anything else she wanted to share. She writes:

"When everything was happening, no one would believe me, and it was a dead-end street anywhere I went. I had discovered Sean online, and seeing that he was a paranormal investigator, I just knew it was what I had been looking for. I know everything happens for a reason, and for some reason, I downloaded that app with that particular song and his contact info.

"When I would have stuff happen or episodes, he was always there when I needed him over the phone or Skype. He got me through what some people wouldn't have been able to. I probably wouldn't be here if it weren't for him."

I pray that nothing returns, and she can go on and live her life in peace with her family. I learned a lot while working with Abby and am thankful for any help I was able to provide her.

The Infiltration

Spirits, Ego, and Entertainment

I have a deep respect for spirits. They are an integral part of my life's work.

This is an important thing for me to state and write about because there are so many different opinions and interpretations of how spirits should be approached in the paranormal. While investigating haunted locations, I have come into contact with all kinds of different spiritual energies. One thing I've learned is that we are all brothers and sisters and that we all come from the same source of light, which is God. We should each strive to treat others as such, whether it be the living or the dead. When going to locations and trying to communicate with those who have passed on, it's important to keep these considerations in mind.

I firmly believe that a key element when it comes to the spirit realm is the intent of the individuals involved in the communication. This is the case whether it's a calm, residential haunting or a location that's full of tormented, trapped souls.

When I think about all the different ways that people die, I realize there are so many different circumstances that can lead to ghosts being present. Sometimes they are attached and don't want to leave their loved ones who are still alive. Sometimes they want justice for something that happened when they were living.

I've encountered spirits who have passed in so many different ways, such as car crashes, drownings, and murder. The first question, of course, is to determine if they are trapped due to their experiences when they were alive. Is it something they can let go of?

Just like people who are still living, spirits can get caught up in dark waves of confusion, obstacles, and negative emotions. Like us, spirits want answers to help get through the darkness.

Sometimes these "ghost souls" that are earthbound can suffer and be blinded by their entrapments. Other times, it's fear that traps these spirits. Perhaps they were bad people in life, or they are filled with guilt because of their actions. I always strive to try to help these spirits return to the light, the unconditional forgiveness of God, whenever possible.

Every action in our lives has energy attached to it, and we will be held accountable for each and every one, be it good or bad. That's where the magical choice that God gave us comes into play—free will.

This gift of free will is one of the reasons the devil hates us so much. Satan and the other fallen angels don't want to give up higher knowledge to creatures who base their decisions on free will and faith in God. I see this as a connection between those still living on the physical plane and the ones who have not let go of human life.

From the beginning, my journey has had a recurring theme: tragic deaths and souls trapped in the earthly realm. These cases are especially intense, particularly if the deaths were at the hands of, or involved, other family members. Imagine a situation where a person kills family members, and then themselves. Afraid of judgment and trapped in spirit form, they may try to hold and control the spirits of the people they killed, stopping them from transiting to heaven, either from spite, anger, or fear.

As investigators and spiritual people, we need to try sympathizing with these spirits. We need to try our best to understand what these people, now spirits, are going through.

We need to connect with them on deeper levels, open ourselves, and listen to their needs.

We should always acknowledge and be humbled by an experience of manifestation or contact with spirits. We demonstrate our willingness to listen and help by connecting with the spirits in ways that show genuine concern and positive intent. In my time in the field, I've found that spirits can often help us as much as we can help them. They do, after all, have unique and different perspectives, as well as views of not only what has occurred at a location, but also the overall influences.

I truly believe, wholeheartedly, that spirits will reciprocate in any way that they can. They can see the color of a living person's aura. This color reveals an individual's intent, so it is a perfect way for them to sense our purpose in contacting them.

This is also one of the reasons that spirits gravitate to children. Children, when they are young, are fresh from the spirit realm and vessels of pure energy. They have their natural spiritual gifts that stay with them until diminished by their environments and the influences around them. Once rational thought processes are impressed on children, they start to close down their intuitive senses.

This makes children, and those who have psychic abilities, able to sense spirits more easily. It also creates an opening that spirits sense and try to use for communication. Of course, there's a flip side to this—negative entities can sense the same thing. It's entities like these, with malevolent intentions, that we must be on guard against. This is also why it's important to pay attention when children say they have "invisible friends" or other unseen beings that they are talking to. While it could be a deceased relative with loving energies, it could also be something much darker, looking for a way in, trying to take advantage of an innocent child.

If more people in the paranormal field would stay aware of these concepts, I believe the community's research would benefit significantly as a whole. Genuine spiritual intent should be at the core of research and work in the paranormal investigation field.

There's another factor that influences the current state of the paranormal field—the meddling of Hollywood and the entertainment industry. Many people now get involved in the paranormal field for the wrong reasons; they want attention and fame. This is an ego-based intention. In my opinion, it actually does much more damage than good. Ego and spirituality don't mix whatsoever. This is one of the reasons that psychics who claimed to have abilities could never win James Randi's million-dollar challenge.

The challenge was set to award one million dollars to anyone who could prove they had psychic ability under laboratory conditions. I believe that people who try to use their gifts for material gain fail in their pursuit. Such gifts come from God, and should be used to help others, not to win money and achieve self-gain and fame.

Of course, it's important to note that Randi's challenge was also rigged in a way that would make it mostly impossible for anyone to succeed. James Randi was a performing magician and gained his fame by pursuing his conflict with a famous psychic, Uri Geller. Randi became a skeptic, and his organization spawned a lot of people, like him, who actively argued that there were no such things as real psychic abilities and ghosts. I feel sorry for these kinds of people; they'll have real surprises in the afterlife!

Randi was capitalizing on the entertainment aspect of being a skeptic. These days, there is a whole range of television shows that capitalize on the opposite, people who believe in ghosts and hauntings.

Now, as many of you know, I've been on television and, yes, there are some nice things about it. I was on Demon Files with my mentor, Ralph Sarchie. The show ran for three episodes on the Travel Channel. Recently, I was on a series called "Ghost Loop," also on the Travel Channel.

I learned a lot from being involved with these two shows. I tried my best to approach these opportunities in a way that was not about ego and was all about helping people spiritually. There are good and bad elements of television. The "Ghost

Loop" team was brought together for the show, and there was a lot of divisiveness, especially when I was selected to be the lead investigator.

Sean and mentor Ralph Sarchie

While working on the show, I pushed hard to have one particular aspect portrayed—the part of praying for spirits for their help and their release. It was important to me to show the spiritual aspect of this work, something that is the most vital component for me. It was a difficult battle, for sure. Hollywood wants drama and conflict: big things that get people's attention and create tension. In other words, ego-based actions and events.

I believe that much of what has happened in the paranormal entertainment industry has given many people who are passionate about the field a bad name. It has also created a lot of conflict between teams, individuals, and even good friends.

Too many people will do whatever it takes to get a television appearance, disregarding, and sometimes betraying their friends and often their own values. People think that getting on that little screen is so important for some reason. Again, it's all about the ego and many of these people don't even realize how much they change after being bitten by the TV fame bug.

Television appearances don't help us find answers or help spirits, and the divisions that entertainment creates have caused countless problems. Aside from losing friends and creating enemies, this kind of pursuit also puts people in danger spiritually.

People should work together in synergy to push forward and find innovations. This would cause great advances in paranormal work, and I hope one day, soon, people will start setting aside the craving for fame and work on things that are much more important.

SHANLEY HOTEL

The Shanley Hotel

Over the course of my time investigating the paranormal, I've stayed in quite a few haunted hotels. Often, I'll seek out these locations since hotels are often hotbeds for paranormal activity. These days, it's pretty easy to find a hotel with ghosts since it's no longer something businesses want to hide. Haunted hotels often do good business just because they are haunted.

When we think about it, it should come as no surprise that so many hotels have ghosts. People from so many different walks of life pass through them. Some of these people are happy; others are suffering mentally, emotionally, and spiritually.

A disturbing number of deaths take place in hotels. Sometimes the deaths are from natural causes, but there are also overdoses, suicides, and even murders. This is not something most people think about when they book a room and check-in. This is not something many people in the hotel industry talk about or advertise, of course, and unless the death is a known historical one, or is linked to a case that received media attention, most people just don't know about them.

Napanoch is a small hamlet in the northern part of my home state of New York. It's in Ulster County on the Shawangunk Ridge National Scenic Byway, part of the Hudson River National Heritage Area.

There's a very haunted hotel in Napanoch called the Shanley Hotel. It's full of unique history and ghosts that have come from many different parts of the building's history and events.

Built on Main street, the hotel was founded by Thomas Ritch in 1845. At the time, Napanoch was a popular vacation spot for those looking for a getaway from the big cities. The railroad made travel to the town easy, and the hotel became popular for its fine food and nice décor.

Ritch sold the hotel in 1851, and it continued as the Hungerford Hotel, still catering to the upper class. The hotel changed hands a few times, and in March 1895, a fire that spread from a nearby house burned the building to the ground. A new building was constructed on the same site, and the hotel was up and running again by November.

In 1906, an Irishman named James Shanley bought the hotel and renamed it the Shanley Hotel. James Shanley added a bowling alley, billiard room, and barbershop to the building. His marriage to Beatrice Rowley took place at the hotel, and the couple was well-loved by the town.

Thomas Edison was a guest at the hotel. Eleanor Roosevelt, who would later be the first lady, was a regular guest at the Shanley, becoming good friends with Beatrice. The Shanley's lived among the upper class and enjoyed the lifestyle associated with it, but tragedies soon struck.

The couple's first child died in 1912 when she was less than six-months-old. Two more children followed, both boys, but neither would live a year. Obviously, losing a child is one of the worst things anyone could go through, and we can only imagine the emotional stain that Beatrice's pain left on the property.

A lot of visitors at the hotel have witnessed a woman in a period dress wandering through the hallways of the hotel. There's a fragrant perfume that's smelled when the woman is present. Is this Beatrice wandering around in mourning from the loss of her children? If it is, she may have yet another reason to be sad.

Beatrice's sister, Esther, died in the hotel in 1918 after

catching influenza. Esther and her husband, John, had moved from New York City to live in the hotel with James and Beatrice, but Esther was constantly homesick for New York. She would sit by the phone for hours, hoping for a call from her friends in the city.

There were other deaths associated with the hotel, too. The hotel barber, Peter Greger, lost his three-year-old daughter, Rosie, when she fell into a nearby well, striking her head on rocks as she plummeted. Greger took his wife and remaining daughter, left his apartment in the hotel, and moved back to Brooklyn.

Rosie had died, at a farm across the street from the hotel, and her body laid there for two hours before she was discovered. People staying in the hotel believe they have encountered her spirit. She manifests as the apparition of a little girl in the hallways of the hotel. Sometimes she hides in the shadows, calling out to people. Maybe she's just being playful, or maybe she's looking for her family who is long gone.

There are a lot of child deaths connected to the Shanley. In September 1915, Dr. Walter Nelson Thayer, Jr. was backing his car out of the alley that ran between his house and the hotel. His five-year-old son, Walter III, jumped on the car's running board and quickly tumbled off again, falling beneath the vehicle and suffering a severe head injury.

Many people believe the ghost of a young boy seen in the hotel's attic is the spirit of little Walter. But the thing is, the boy didn't die from the accident, so exactly who is the spirit that people see? The ghost is called Jonathan, but it isn't clear where the nickname came from. Perhaps there was another child that died at the hotel whose story is lost in history; either way, the ghost is quite a mystery.

When prohibition came to the United States, a speakeasy was established in the hotel to cater to those looking for illegal booze. Peter Greger's apartment later became a bordello to fulfill patrons' other desires.

James Shanley was actively involved with bootlegger John Powers, and kept booze hidden beneath the bar down a hidden trapdoor. The hotel was raided in February 1932, and Shanley and Powers were arrested. Neither of the men did prison time, and some believe this may be due to the Shanley's connection with Eleanor and President Roosevelt.

People believe the ghost of John Powers is still at the Shanley Hotel, too. Maybe he enjoyed his time there so much that he never wanted to leave, even in the afterlife.

James Shanley, himself, died of a massive heart attack in 1937. The entire town of Napanoch mourned his passing, a mark of how deeply he was loved by the community. Eleanor Roosevelt sent a letter to her friend, Beatrice, expressing her sadness, writing that she was sorry that she'd heard about the death too late to attend the funeral.

Beatrice sold the hotel to Allen H. Hazen. Under Hazen's ownership, one of the hotel's rooms gained its nickname—the Silent Room. According to the story, if Hazen had had too many encounters with spirits, that is, the spirits found in a bottle, then staff members and guests would tiptoe around the room while he slept it off.

The Shanley Hotel changed hands many times over the years but was closed down and abandoned in 1991.

In 2005, Salvatore Nicosia, a man, said to have vision and a heart of gold, purchased the Shanley. Sal, as he was known, didn't know about the ghost stories associated with the hotel but knew about its history and wanted to bring it back to life. Sal reopened the hotel in 2007 and operated it until his passing in 2016. The hotel was condemned and closed down again in December 2017 but reopened under new management in 2018.

I never got to meet Sal, but I've heard so many great stories about him that I feel like I know him. He was well-liked by people in the paranormal community and was passionate about the hotel, its history, and its spirits. He did an amazing job breathing new life into the hotel and giving the spirits a comfortable place. I'm sure the ghosts of the Shanley loved Sal as much as he loved the hotel since he had restored many of the building's former features.

I'd had my eye on the Shanley for a long time and always

wanted to investigate it. The timing never quite worked out for me to get there, and the hotel closed, then reopened under a new owner. When I saw that they were taking guests again, I quickly booked a room. I wasn't going to risk missing out on the place anymore.

The Historic Shanley Hotel

Driving up to the hotel, the first sight of the building gave me a nice, creepy, foreboding vibe, exactly what I expected from a historic, haunted hotel.

I walked in the front door and took the place in, feeling its energy right away. I soon learned that guests must sign a waiver before staying the night in one of the rooms. This is for the protection of the hotel staff, so they aren't blamed for anything the hotel's spirits do.

I met the Shanley's new owner, Kelly, and her friend, Kimberly. They were very welcoming, beyond friendly, and right away started telling me about experiences they'd had in the hotel. It's always a pleasure to meet like-minded people who are passionate about the subject of the paranormal.

Kelly had been an investigator herself, spending time at the hotel when Sal owned it. When she had a chance to take over the Shanley, she jumped at it. It was great that a person so passionate about the paranormal had taken over a haunted, historic hotel! I saw the same heart and love for the site from Kelly that everyone said Sal had had for the place. Kelly is friendly to the spirits, and they seem to treat her the same.

As other people started to show up for the night at the Shanley, we shared experiences and good conversation, getting psyched up to see what the evening would bring.

We started our investigation in the area that was once a bordello. The rooms are in the upstairs back section of the hotel. There are three rooms that face outwards toward a smaller main room next to the stairs. As we sat down, we put some devices out, including an EMF meter to detect electromagnetic energy. EMF meters are used to detect fluctuations in the electromagnetic field and can indicate the presence of ghosts. Spirits can use electrical energy in various ways, draining batteries and electrical equipment in order to gather energy to communicate or even manifest.

I also turned on an SB7 Spirit Box to open communication. I like the SB7 a lot since it gives spirits the opportunity for real-time communication when they are able to come through and use the radio frequencies to form words or even phrases.

The room I was sitting in is called Anna's room, and it's believed she was one of the ladies of the night who worked in the bordello during its heyday. Right away, there were sexual references coming over the device. I started to get a cold chill over my lap and on the left side of my body. Was this one of the working girls wanting to see if I was a customer? I got a weird spider web-like feeling that glided over the left side of my face as this was happening. A female voice said my name over the spirit box, and more sexual comments were spoken. The voice seemed like it was trying to flirt with me.

The whole situation was kind of comical. Kim and Kelly were in the room, and they were getting a real kick out of the interaction as it unfolded. There were a few other people present too, and they all thought it was funny. I've had female spirits try this type of thing before, but this situation was unique, and

I was laughing about it as well.

Another spirit said to be in the room is that of a man named Frank. He's known to be a malicious entity, and Kelly said she had been choked by the spirit of Frank. Frank's name has come through on numerous investigations at the hotel, and there are implications that he wants to be in control of the female spirits who are there. This desire to control seems to extend to living women who come into the area. There are other odd sounds that are frequently heard in the bordello area, making it one of the hotel's hotspots.

After the ladies of the evening started to calm down in their pursuit of me, we left the area to check out another part of the hotel. We headed down to the basement, another area of reported high paranormal activity.

As one would expect, the basement is dark, musty, and smelled, well, like a stinky basement. Some people believe there's a portal in this part of the hotel, an entry point into the other world, or a place where darker entities can come into our world. I certainly felt the heaviness of the space. There's an uncomfortable feeling of being watched when in the basement. To the right of the basement is an old wooden door. Kelly said it was once used as a morgue sometime in the building's past.

The spirit box was going, and the voices of children started to come through. There was also a male voice that was very negative, telling us to get out and leave. I felt a dark presence and I wasn't sure if it was from the hotel itself or from somewhere else. I thought about some of the stories associated with the building, rumors of the Irish mob being active around the Shanley crossed my mind. What deaths had occurred at the property that had been long forgotten?

All this time, the EMF meter was taking hits, indicating that something was certainly present. The voice mentioned "portal," indicating that there may, indeed, be a portal in the basement. The communication wound down, and no other information came in, so we decided to wrap up and try a different area of the hotel.

We headed up to the second floor and went into a room

adjacent to the one that Sal, the previous owner, had used. The energy was good, not heavy or oppressive at all, and we started getting references to Sal and the hotel as a whole.

I was loving how much activity was coming through at this amazing place! I've stayed in a lot of haunted hotels, and I've often been restricted to just the room I booked for the night, so it was great to get to explore the whole building this time around.

We made our way to the hotel's third floor. It was almost like a different world. Kelly told us the third floor had angry spirits. Allegedly, a woman had killed herself there, and the whole space exuded a lot of energies. The rooms stay empty on the third floor, and it retains a creepy vibe.

While in one room doing a session with the spirit box. A male voice came through; clearly it wasn't a nice spirit. Suddenly, one of the women in the group said she couldn't breathe, and she quickly left the room. As it turned out, Kelly had experienced the same thing in this room on a previous occasion. Why was there such dark energy up here? The whole thing made me wonder if the area had also been used for bordello activity at some point.

These are the highlights of my first night at the Shanley Hotel, one filled with lots of activity and varied responses. Since that experience, I've returned to the site a number of times.

On another investigation at the hotel, I found myself again in the bordello area with a female spirit, perhaps Anna, communicating and being very flirtatious through the spirit box. It seemed the ghost of this woman had taken a real liking to me! The more I visited the hotel, the more she communicated with me.

Kelly opened up another room that I'd never been in before. This one was on the first floor. There are pews from an old church in the room, as well as some chairs. We sat down to see what would turn up in the room. This space was more oppressive and heavier than other rooms of the hotel.

We had a spirit box running, and I was looking around the room, sort of expecting something to manifest. At that moment, I saw a black ball of spirit energy right next to a friend of mine,

Miranda, who was sitting nearby. Usually, when I see black energy manifest like this, it's not a good sign and is usually something very dark and evil.

I told Miranda to be careful, and I let her know what I was seeing. White noise was running on the device, and we were listening for a response. There were two other women in the room, and they both heard a loud, audible growl. It didn't come from the device; it somehow manifested out of thin air. The girls were shaken up and immediately got up to change their seats, moving to a different area of the room.

Miranda had heard the growl, too. All of this was right after I'd seen the black energy manifest near her. The thing was, right before this happened, while sitting in the room, we were all having a conversation, and Miranda mentioned how much she disliked growling sounds. The room had gotten very uncomfortable, and we decided to make our way out and go to another part of the hotel.

Miranda discovered that she had captured the image of a strange shadow anomaly darting across the hallway. The shadow manifested in a video she took of the stairs leading to the second floor. Several of us examined the video, and we could find nothing to explain it. The mass was about the size of a child. Could this be the spirit of one of the children that reportedly haunt the hotel?

The unexplainable video was a nice piece of evidence captured that night, and we were inspired to investigate more to see what else we could catch.

We made our way down to the basement, an area that always felt heavy and creepy. A friend of mine, Howie, was with me this time. We went into the area that had once been a morgue. I looked over to my left to the area where bodies had been stored. I rubbed my eyes because I saw two yellow eyes peeking at me from the shadows in the area. What had I just seen? Whatever it was, it didn't feel like something good.

I was running an infra-red camera at the time and witnessed a white anomaly do a circle and go over to Howie. Later review of the footage revealed no explainable reason for the light manifestation. Something was trying to make itself known in the basement.

Nothing else came up, so we left the basement and headed up to the third floor. Several of us sat down in the first room at the top right of the stairs. Right away, we were getting constant hits on our EMF detectors. We sat down in a circle and continued to communicate with the spirits.

As we were sitting there, I looked out and into an adjacent room. I suddenly shouted out because I saw two glowing, yellow eyes staring at us from the other room.

Eric, another man in the group, quickly replied that he'd seen them as well. Eric described the eyes as two yellow slots floating in mid-air, staring down at us.

This was exactly what I had seen just beforehand down in the basement. What was this thing, and why was it following me around the hotel? Had this thing come through the portal said to be in the basement? I talked to Eric about the yellow eyes, confirming some points of what he'd seen. It's always great to have confirmation of a paranormal event from another witness. We investigated the hotel into the early hours of the morning, with plenty of continued activity.

I've found myself very drawn to the Shanley Hotel. No matter how many times I visit, I leave wanting to spend more time there, to probe deeper and longer to see what other kinds of interactions will occur and what the next startling piece of evidence will be.

I've dug into the hotel's history while continuing to investigate and learn from a paranormal perspective. In fact, the Shanley has been the location of a couple of the most unique and strange paranormal experiences that I've had in my time as an investigator.

A couple of weeks after one of my visits to the hotel, I had an incident that led me to believe that a spirit from the place was connected to me. I was dozing off in my bed one night when I went into a lucid visionary experience. I could see a blurry scene that was playing out in the vision. I wasn't just seeing the place. I was physically feeling what was occurring as well.

I could see two women, both were wearing old-fashioned period clothing. They were giggling at me. Both of them were touching me sexually while laughing to themselves. It seemed like they were having some fun with the situation! In the background, a record player was going, playing what was clearly old-fashioned music, though I couldn't pinpoint exactly what it was. This all went on for several minutes, then I suddenly jumped awake.

Over time, I've learned to differentiate between a random dream experience and something that has a spiritual quality. I knew right away there was more to this experience than a simple dream.

The two women were both brunettes. I could only partially see one of the girl's faces, but from what I saw, she seemed like a very pretty woman. Was this Anna still trying her best to treat me like one of her gentlemen customers from the bordello?

I'd already had the feeling that Anna had taken a particular interest and liking to me, and this incident further confirmed it. One would think that discussing these kinds of experiences would be uncomfortable, but I believe it's important to be able to discuss such things in order to grow and learn, regardless of how strange or awkward the situations may be.

I had another experience that I believe involved the spirit of Anna. This time, the experience was, well, very intense in a different way. I was in bed again, but this time I was watching television. Out of nowhere, a strong smell overcame me. It was the smell of a woman's private parts. The smell was very pronounced and unmistakable. I was thinking to myself; you've got to be kidding me!!! I was looking around the room, trying to figure out how and why this overpowering smell was all around me out of nowhere.

I wasn't sure if I should get up out of bed and bless my room or what. I thought about it for a few seconds, then turned on a recorder, sitting in silence, just letting it run. I wanted to see if I could pick up any EVPs.

I shut the recorder off and hit playback to see if I had captured anything. I did for sure, and I couldn't believe what I heard. A female voice said, "lick my p***y."

I've never had anything like this happen. It was crazy, funny, and mind-blowing all at the same time. This was completely off the grid for me. Despite the craziness of the situation, I had a strong intuition about it—I just knew that the manifestation was from the Shanley Hotel.

Just to be on the safe side, I got up and did a blessing of my apartment. I felt confident the incident was connected to one of the ladies of the evening from the bordello rooms at the Shanley, but I wanted to be safe in case a succubus had somehow found its way to my home.

A succubus is a demonic spawn that sexually attacks its victims. A succubus takes the form of a beautiful and attractive woman who comes to a male victim and lures them into sexual encounters, all the while draining their energy and life force away. They are extremely dangerous and evil creatures.

An incubus is the male version of these demons, and it takes the form of an attractive man. The incubus preys on female victims in a sexual way, still working towards the same goal of draining life force and energy away.

On another trip to the Shanley, I joined up last minute with a group of people who were also involved with the paranormal. Once again, I found myself with a great group of people who were all passionate about the paranormal.

I told Kelly about my weird bedtime experiences with what I believed was the spirit of Anna. Needless to say, she got quite a kick out of the story and had a good laugh. After hearing my story, it was a no-brainer to start in the bordello. Right away, the sexual comments started coming in over the spirit box again, and there were references to Anna. One person in the room said he felt a strange burning sensation on his arms, and we wondered if something was trying to scratch him. We checked out the spot on his arms with a flashlight, and although it was a bit red, there was no clear indication of anything. Oddly though, one of the devices mentioned his arms a few moments later. I'm not sure if there was, indeed, an attempt to scratch him or if the spirits were just echoing our group's conversation about his arms. Either way, it was an interesting confirmation of their conscious presence in the room.

After this, the energies seemed to turn dark. Verbal responses from the spirit box were stating that something "dark" was with us in the room. Kelly said this was unusual, as they don't normally get mentions of dark energies in the area. She did say that on occasion, some of the spirits were somewhat tricky and would make comments about the devil and such to frighten or mess with people doing investigations.

I've seen this kind of thing before. If the spirits are not interested in communicating or being bothered, or if there's someone present who they don't care for, they can make it seem like there's a dark and negative spirit present in an effort to drive the people out of their spaces.

Kelly had a new device to try out that night, a device that had been gaining a lot of popularity in the paranormal field—a music box with a motion sensor attached. This device projects a beam that, if broken by something unseen, sets off the box causing music to play.

We set the device up in Anna's room to see if we could get any reactions. Sure enough, the box started going off constantly with no one in the room. Obviously, one of the ghosts in the area liked being able to trigger music.

Later that night, we found ourselves on the hotel's main floor and decided to try some EVP sessions. Sitting in complete darkness, I started a recorder and let it run, asking some questions here and there, leaving time between for the spirits to answer. After several minutes of this, I stopped recording and hit playback on the device. The responses that came through were again dark in nature.

The demon, Beelzebub, was mentioned. We were all creeped out by the name being mentioned, and it wasn't something we expected. Next came a very clear phrase, "He knows you're a demonologist." Everyone was shocked and excited at the same time. It was amazing how clear the voice was. The vibe in the room became heavier for a few moments, but then, whatever it was seemed to back off.

These kinds of energy waves are not uncommon in the paranormal. Frequently, communication comes on strongly, and then suddenly fades away or stops completely. This even happens with my intuitive abilities; they can peak and reach high points and then flatten out suddenly. Sometimes information comes in non-stop, and at other times it's hard to tap in at all.

A lot of things affect this. One factor is the cycle of the moon. Our planet is mostly water, and the moon affects water heavily. A good example is the moon's effect on the oceans' tides. Since our bodies are made up of so much water, it would make sense that we're affected on personal levels by the moon and its cycles.

Paranormal researchers believe water is often a conduit for energy and paranormal activity. Science might not accept such ideas yet, but I do believe there's something to the concept.

We finally made our way down to the basement. As is the case every time I'm in the area, the energy was heavy and oppressive, and there was the feeling of being watched. Later review of audio and video evidence picked up a voice warning me about going into the basement. This time, there was an audible, nasty growl as I entered the area.

I stepped into the old morgue, the place where I had seen the weird glowing eyes looking at me. It was a creepy feeling, and I felt an evil presence in the room watching me. At this time, I was running a live feed on my periscope, and it suddenly had a weird glitch. Later, on review of the footage, I looked at the time when the glitch occurred. At that moment, there was a shadow that appeared on the screen. But it wasn't just a normal shadow. This one had what looked like horns and a pair of yellow eyes that were staring in my direction! Whatever this thing was, it wanted to make it very clear to me that it was there, and that it was watching me. It had certainly accomplished this!

I would later learn that this thing with the yellow eyes was something that was apparently following me to other locations I investigated. I now believe this entity had nothing, in particular, to do with the Shanley; rather, it seems to be connected to the pig-like creature I encountered in Borg's Woods in New Jersey.

In fact, evidence from spirit boxes directly stated that the entity was the demonic thing from those haunted woods. Apparently, I had made an enemy in the demonic realm because of my prayers and work in helping trapped souls. This pig demon wanted to harass me and make it clear that I was on its list. It wanted to take revenge on me for continuing to do God's work in the physical world.

I'm sure these tactics of following me around to other locations and continuing to make its presence known were meant to intimidate me and try to make me afraid of continuing my work. Too bad, I have no intention of stopping what I do and will continue to pray for lost spirits and those seeking help and forgiveness.

After some more dark responses, I'd had enough of the basement that night, and we all went out and back up to the hotel's third floor. Once there, the devices began spitting out responses; something nasty seemed to be in the room. A male voice started coming through, and it was addressing me directly. It was responding to my questions and statements and said, "That's your woman," and "You can have both of 'em."

This was shocking because I had mentioned the story of the two female spirits I had encountered in my home after being at the Shanley. I believed the two spirits were from the bordello, and this male voice now confirmed my suspicions. Perhaps this spirit was the old bordello boss.

Later review of footage from this session revealed white light anomalies that manifested on my left side. Around the time this was happening, I had a cold chill pass over me. Was this the spirit of Anna trying once again to make contact and interact with me?

The spirits of Anna and Frank continued to make their presence known during the night's investigation. These two spirits, in particular, are frequently around me whenever I visit the hotel, and it seems we've developed a real connection over time. Frank doesn't say a whole lot, but Anna, of course, is always very flirtatious and loves to throw out sexual references and comments. It continues to be both shocking and funny.

It was another eventful time at the Shanley, and as always, it was hard to leave the place, but it wasn't long before I made a return trip.

My next investigation at the Shanley was a bit different. Usually, there's a number of people at the hotel wandering around and investigating. This time, however, we had a much smaller group. The owner, Kelly, was there, of course, and I had brought a friend of mine named Julie, but that was it.

The pace was very different this time, and so was the atmosphere. We did the usual rounds in our normal order. In the bordello, right off the bat, a male voice came over the spirit box and said, "Watching Julie." Clearly, at least one of the spirits wanted her to know that it was paying attention to her. Frank and Anna came in right away, too, with their standard types of communications.

Back on the main floor, something kept saying, "Ouija." Three of us sat there and heard the word clearly, not once, but numerous times. I wondered why the box kept saying this over and over. No reference to a Ouija board had ever come up in my time investigating the hotel. I asked Julie if she had ever played with a Ouija board, and she replied that she had once when she was a little girl. So again, it didn't make sense that the reference kept repeating.

I kept getting intuitive flashes related to the reported portal in the hotel's basement, and I thought it odd that numerous references to a Ouija board kept coming up during this time. Kelly couldn't make sense of the reference either, and I wondered what was at play. Was something negative trying to get us to use a Ouija board so it could get through the portal? Perhaps someone had used a board on the premises recently, and it had created some kind of connection.

We were getting hits on several of the devices and we were soon drawn down to the basement. It felt like we were being lured to the portal area, but we couldn't just ignore the indications that were coming up. Clearly, it needed further investigation.

Once in the basement, we set up a flashlight to see if the

spirits could manipulate it and cause it to turn on. Then we started an EVP session. We took turns asking questions, and while doing the session, we heard audible conversations going on around us. We all looked at each other each, asking if the other had heard the voices. We all confirmed hearing them.

Typically, sprits speak on a frequency that we can't hear with our own ears. This is why investigators use recorders that can pick up those frequencies the human ear can't tune into alone. On rare occasions, investigators may hear audible disembodied voices, and I have to say when it happens, it's a very special experience, especially when several people all have the experience at the same time!

For some reason, this happened several times that night. Maybe it was the timing, or maybe it was just the right mix of people. It was hard to distinguish what, exactly, was being said, but at one point, we heard a child's voice make two quick humming noises. I thought it almost sounded like an owl, though Kelly said it sounded different to her. I was recording with my phone when the sound was heard. On playback, the two humming noises came through very clearly. Listening to the recording, we all agreed it sounded like a little boy, and Kelly told us that the spirit of a little boy had been known to hang around down in the basement. The ghost boy is known as Jamie.

We continued to hear audible conversations going on in the basement. We were all blown away by this and tried our best to debunk it, but there was no explanation for where the voices were coming from. To me, it felt like the spirits were active and in full swing, trying to make their presence known. The humming sound was captured on the recorder once again. The experience was eye-opening for Julie, who couldn't believe the level of activity. Multiple things were occurring at the same time. We noticed one of the EMF meters taking hits, and there seemed to be something going on around the flashlight. We asked if the spirit of the little boy could answer some questions and use the flashlight to respond. We wanted to know if his name was Jamie. When we asked, the light came on, confirming for us that Jamie was his name. We also asked him if there was a scary spirit in the room with us, to which he responded, "Yes." Whatever else was in the basement, the spirit of the little boy didn't like it.

Next, I heard a woman's voice. I immediately turned around to Julie and Kelly, asking if they had heard the woman. We had all heard the voice, and we sat about trying to determine where it had come from. We all agreed the voice sounded like that of an older woman, but again, we could find no logical explanation or source to explain the voice.

We all had different opinions on where we thought the voice was centered. One of us thought it came from the morgue; another thought it was in the area where the portal was supposed to be. We concluded that it was probably sourced in the middle of all three of us.

When disembodied voices manifest, it's difficult to determine their locations in a physical sense. I've experienced this before when I've been alone and heard disembodied voices. Often, they sound as if they are coming from across the room, from behind, or even from the next room over. Some of this is due to the quality of the voices and the fact that they are speaking from the spirit realm. Because of this, it's not uncommon to have a hard time distinguishing words or hearing the voices clearly.

This kind of activity continued for some time that night. Another odd factor is that while Kelly and I both had recorders running, my recorder was the only one that picked up the voices.

Again, this is one of the curious things that can happen during investigations, and there's really no way to explain it. Maybe the spirits were being tricksters and causing this effect just to screw with us. Of course, it makes no logical sense since the recorders were in the same room and close together. One would think that both recorders would pick up the frequencies that the spirits were speaking on.

Using the flashlight for responses, we asked the little boy, Jamie, some other questions. Kelly asked him if he would like a toy. As soon as she asked this question, I heard the phrase, "Choo Choo Train" in my head. This brought me back to the sound the little boy had made that we'd all heard audibly, and that was captured on the recorder.

We immediately asked Jamie to turn the flashlight on if he wanted a train. Sure enough, the flashlight lit up! After this exchange, things began to cool down in the basement, and it seemed the energy there was fizzling out, so we took a break to let things settle.

Julie and I ended up going up to the third floor. As soon as we sat down, we started hearing strange sounds all around us. Once again, the ghost box started making references to Ouija boards.

There were other, aggressive words coming out of the box. I had the feeling that something up there didn't like Julie and perhaps wanted to frighten her, or worse, harm her. We had various devices on at this time, and I asked out loud, "Is it Julie, you want to harm?" Right away, the flashlight came on.

I felt that a male spirit in the room was definitely trying to scare Julie. I'm not sure why this was the case, but I told her to remain calm. Spirits can see our auras and sense fear and other states. They will try to take advantage of people's emotional states whenever they can, and darker energies feed off negative emotions like fear. This being the case, it's always important to try to stay calm and balanced during situations when an entity is trying to make you a target. Around this time, my recorder picked up an EVP that said either, "I know that guy," or "I know that girl." Despite numerous playbacks, the last word was difficult to distinguish, but it appeared that something seemed to "know" either Julie or me and was stating it. I decided to try to get clarification of what was being said by asking for a response on one of the other devices.

I told the spirits, "If you said, 'I know that girl,' make the flashlight go off or make the MEL meter go off." There was no response, and I waited a few moments before asking the next question. This time I repeated the request to light up the flashlight or the MEL meter if the statement had been, "I know that guy." This time, the meter went off, confirming the communication.

This is another demonstration of the use of multiple pieces of equipment to confirm points of communication and evidence. The voice on the recorder was mostly clear, but that last word wasn't, and it would have changed the nature of the statement if it was the other way around.

We decided to try a different area of the hotel and headed to a room that was purportedly the site of a woman's suicide. Julie started to feel strange and got slightly dizzy as soon as we approached the room.

As we were walking down the hallway towards the room, we both heard a loud, disembodied scream! It wasn't just a low sound either; it was a bloodcurdling scream that would make the hair go up on the back of your neck.

The scream was unnerving and sounded like someone being tormented or killed. Whatever the scream was in response to, it was clearly painful and horrible. Out of all the various voices and sounds we heard in the hotel that night, this one was by far the most disturbing and troubling, to say the least.

After taking a deep breath, I turned the spirit box back on to see if we could get some further information. There was a voice talking, but it was hard to hear words again. I asked out loud if there was anyone that would like me to say a prayer. A response quickly came out of the ghost box, saying, "Pray."

I stopped and said a prayer out loud, and when I completed it, a voice from the spirit box said, "Amen." I had the sense that a female spirit was present and trying to cross over into the light. I saw the image of a white dove, my personal symbol to confirm this.

After my prayer, things got quiet. Even the spirit box had little coming out of it, basically only white noise. It's a strange thing, but this happens often after I've said a prayer and felt like a spirit was crossing over to heaven.

I've spent a lot of time at the Shanley Hotel, and as often as I go, I always leave knowing that I'll soon be back again. I feel like I have a personal relationship and connection to the spirits that haunt the old place. Some of them are there simply because of their personal love of the hotel. Some of the energies may be residual. Either way, there's always a nice variety of interactions that occur at the location, and I've no doubt it will continue to be like this. There's really no place quite like the Shanley and no other hotel that is so well-suited for paranormal investigators. It's such a great experience each and every time, and on each visit, I add more pieces to the paranormal puzzle that the hotel presents.

If you have any interest in haunted locations and the paranormal, I highly recommend you check out the Shanley.

It's important to pray for lost spirits to help them cross over.

The mysterious Cabin on 360

The Spider Demon

There are plenty of well-known haunted locations to investigate, but even still, I'm always looking for new places that aren't so hyped from television and years of attention. Sometimes I find locations from my own research, other times from people who contact me. This was the case, one day, when my friend, Dave Spinks, called to tell me about a location he had just learned about in Mechanicsville, Virginia.

Dave was one of the people mentioned in my first book; we've investigated a number of haunted locations together over the years. It's always great to connect with other people who are passionate about investigating the paranormal, and when Dave started telling me about the location, I was ready to go even before hearing all the details.

I learned that the location was a cabin where very unsettling things were happening to people. Reportedly, there were at least three different potential hotspots on the property: the main cabin (which had possibly been a brothel at some point in history), a rancher next door (where the sadistic rape and murder of a little girl had occurred at the hands of her step-brother, no less), and a forested area that had been a battleground.

The list of things that people have experienced at the location is long: physical attacks, such as scratches and pushes, disembodied voices, phantom smells and feelings of nausea, shadow figures, and much more.

The place sounded interesting, and I was ready to hit the road to investigate. While driving to Virginia, I wondered what the investigation would bring. What kind of entities were running around the property? What level of spiritual energy would I encounter? With all the varied reports, I had to consider that there was likely something dark infesting the place. I was slightly anxious, and, of course, excited to be on the way to a new location.

I arrived at the cabin after dark and connected with Dave. We met the curators of the location, Ryan and Dennis, a pair of real gentlemen. I found out that Dennis was very knowledgeable about the history and the hauntings of the cabin. Ryan also knew a lot about the location and had a special connection to it. As he told me:

"The Cabin on 360 is a very special place to me. It's more than just a haunted location. When Dennis Estlock and I first decided to investigate the cabin and the brick house, we wanted to have a place where we could practice different methods of paranormal investigating. We wanted to set up a paranormal laboratory, so to speak, where we could teach our team different investigating techniques.

"We knew the brick house was active, and we were planning on using the cabin as a home base. But soon we found out that both places were active, and not long after that, we discovered the woods behind the cabin were active, as well.

"Dennis and I would spend hours at the cabin gathering evidence. At first, we had invited only a few select people to come out and investigate with us. Once we realized how active the location was, we decided to start inviting some of our friends to come out and investigate with us. We figured it would be good to get some fresh faces in the house to see if they got as much activity as we did. Let me tell you, the houses did not disappoint!

"We knew we had something special, and our original idea of just using the houses as a training area slowly began to change. Our first public investigation was in November 2016. I was definitely nervous because I had been talking about how great the cabin was, and I did not want to disappoint the people who came out for the event. You know, you do these events, and sometimes things just kind of run together, but sometimes, things stand out and what stood out to me about this event was the feeling I got when people realized that all this ghost stuff is real. The look in a person's eyes when that light goes on, and they know all this is real, it's a great feeling.

"I have had so many awesome experiences at the cabin, both personal and paranormal. As far as personal experiences are concerned, the number one has to be meeting my girlfriend, Ange Parker. There's a backstory to Ange and the cabin. About fourteen years ago, Ange had a daughter, Kimmie. The cabin was a hair and nail salon then. A friend had gotten her a spa day after she had the baby. The nail salon was in the downstairs back room of the cabin. She told me she looked out of the window while she was waiting for her nails to dry and saw two dark shadow figures in the yard behind the brick house, one tall and one short. She did not know any of the history behind what happened inside the brick house. She didn't know what to think about it.

"Fast forward to the present, and we had been talking on an internet dating site. We had become friends on Facebook, but we had not met in person yet. Out of the blue, she messaged me and asked about the cabin. She said that she'd been having dreams about the place and was wondering if she could come out. Of course, I said, "Yes," and we picked a time to meet up. When we met, there was instant chemistry. I felt like I had known her my whole life. It was an amazing feeling, and we have not gone more than one or two days apart since. I don't know what caused her to have dreams about the cabin, or what prompted her to contact me, but I have a feeling there is something supernatural involved."

I found Ryan's story so interesting. Over the years, I've heard similar stories about people who met because of a paranormal location or haunting. Often, lifelong friendships or relationships are formed due to the paranormal. It's certainly one of the more positive things that can come, even out of dark hauntings. To me, it's further proof of something divine, a way for God to send people into your life that can help, heal, and be companions along life's path.

Ryan had a paranormal story about the cabin to share, too.

"During Christmastime, we like to do a toy drive at the cabin for Toys for Tots. We want to do our part to help the children in the area have a Merry Christmas. We take our investigations seriously, but since it was Christmas, we were more jovial and joking around. We had been investigating upstairs in the brick rancher. We had a big group upstairs in Melissa's room and decided to split the group up with the females staying upstairs (to make Melissa more comfortable) and the men going downstairs to the basement.

"We had a father who had come with his daughter, and they did not want to split up, so she came downstairs with us. When we got downstairs, we were talking and laughing. We had not settled down yet to start the investigation. We had not turned on the lights downstairs, so it was pretty dark. I remember hearing some of the guys laughing about something, but I also heard what sounded like somebody crying.

"I soon realized the sound was coming from right next to me. The girl who had come downstairs with her dad was staring and frantically pointing at the steps leading upstairs. Her dad was trying his best to calm her down, but she kept crying and saying, "It's looking at me. It's right there!" My first instinct was to get her out of there and to find Dennis. Once we got her outside, she began to calm down, and she told us what she saw.

"She said that when she looked back towards the steps, she saw a tall, dark shadow figure standing behind the steps. The basement was dark, but there are windows, and the light from the street makes it so you can see. I know she saw something because I could hear the fear in her voice.

"Once we got her back to the cabin and she spoke with Dennis, she was able to get her composure back, and she went right back into the basement to confront what was down there. She has not had any problems since then, but she is not the first, or the last person, that the entity in the basement has affected. There is something dark downstairs in the brick house, and we tell people all the time to be careful because it can affect even the most experienced investigator[s].

"The cabin is a unique place because it is both welcoming and very dark at the same time. There is so much history jam-packed on this relatively small piece of land. Like I say, if you are ever in the area and want to come and see for yourself, we are always here."

As I listened to Ryan and Dennis tell me about their experiences at the location, I could already feel what was coming. I knew there were energies there, waiting, and it would be interesting to see what happened over the next two nights exploring the site.

The guys had a strange image of a face they'd captured on a thermal camera. When they captured it, they had been getting references to a specific demon. When they researched the name, they found that the depiction in the demonology book they referenced looked just like the face they had captured on camera.

I wondered if there was, indeed, something demonic at the location. Was it feeding on the suffering of the humans who had met with tragedy on the property, drawn by the various events, or had someone called the entity in, either on purpose or by mistake?

A quick tour of the rancher was up next. This brick house is where the purported rape and murder had taken place. It was a horrible story involving a young girl who was raped and murdered, then pulled out of the home's window and taken into the forest behind the house.

I could tell right away there was a lot of evil in the building. With my first steps towards it, I could sense the darkness. The feeling was both anxious and ominous, and I wasn't fully sure what to expect that night.

As soon as Dennis unlocked the door, I was hit. The level of oppressive energy from the place was one of the worst and heaviest that I had ever felt. One of the rooms made me feel dizzy and disrupted with my equilibrium. For me, this is usually a sign that there's a portal or gateway in the space. The whole house was nauseating.

Next, Dennis led the way to the basement. There was the same heavy feeling there, and on top of that, there was the distinct feeling of being watched. It was not a good feeling at all.

The brick rancher at the Cabin on 360 site

While Dennis was talking about the demonic face caught on thermal imaging, I looked over to the wall to the left of the stairs. Crawling on the wall was a spider.

Now, I'm not a fan of spiders. Not at all. And this thing wasn't even a normal spider that might be hanging around a window or something. We're not talking about an itsy-bitsy spider. This thing had to be the size of an orange.

I told Dennis that there was no way in hell that I was coming down into the basement later in the pitch dark, knowing that damn thing was crawling around somewhere. It was hair-raising to think about that thing creeping around in the dark. I managed to get by the spider and back upstairs. It was time to get ready to investigate.

I got Dave, and we went back to unload the equipment from our cars. We would be sleeping upstairs in the cabin and had inflatable mattresses to sleep on. Once everything was ready, we based our equipment on the first floor of the cabin and set up for a live stream.

We started with an SB7 Spirit Box to get things going. Right away, responses started coming in. The voices didn't seem nice, and they didn't seem happy that we were there. Curses and evil references started coming in. One of the voices started targeting Dave, and this caused him to get more forceful. Dave suddenly made a loud, grunting noise and bent over, holding his stomach. "Are you okay, man?" I asked.

"No," he responded, "I feel like something just hit me."

Dave headed for the front door and went outside. I grabbed a camera and followed. There he was on the cabin's porch, bent over the railing heaving and throwing up.

"Are you serious, man?" I asked. I couldn't believe something like this was happening so quickly after starting to investigate. Dave was choking and gagging, trying to get a few words out when he could.

"Felt as if someone just punched me in the gut," he managed to say.

I still had the spirit box running during this episode, and a nasty male voice shouted out, "He deserved that."

This all confirmed my suspicion that we were dealing with some very serious energies. We took a break to make sure that Spinks was okay and able to continue. He still didn't feel right as we sat down and discussed some things. Dave needed a longer break to clear himself from the attack. Dennis was there with us, and he and I decided to go over to the brick rancher while Spinks relaxed a bit out of the energy of this dark place.

When Dennis and I entered the house, the negative energy of the place hit me once again. Nausea, oppression, despair, it was a mix of energies so heavy and almost overwhelming. We went upstairs and did some spirit box sessions, receiving some interesting responses. I could sense something very evil in the place. The presence was something I knew I had to be on guard against; it pressed in as if it was trying to put me in a daze.

We decided to go back down to the basement, down where the giant spider had been earlier. I admit, in the back of my mind, I was worried about one of those things dropping down on me in the darkness. It was so creepy to think about, creepier than the negative entities that were running around inside the place. It might not make sense, but go figure, spiders, especially ones the size of f*#@ing saucers really disturb me.

Dennis and I walked around in the basement, getting some bits of communication here and there on the ghost box. As we peeked around the middle of the basement, I suddenly felt something crawling on my neck. It felt like someone's fingers moving across my skin. I yelped out really loud and jumped around. Dennis went into fight or flight mode, thinking that I was possessed or something. I told him, immediately, what had happened and what I had felt on my neck.

Dennis got a good laugh out of the situation, but I had to wonder, what exactly had happened? What caused the feeling? Was this the evil entity lurking around the site? Was it trying to trigger a response, knowing that I don't like spiders?

I am well-aware that the demonic likes to use fear as a tool and as a way to take energy from people. I had a lot of questions, and it had been a hell of a night that went by fast. We decided to wrap up after the excitement of the phantom spider on my neck.

Later that night, Dave and I were sleeping upstairs in the cabin. During the night, we were awakened by banging noises. I sat up and listened, hearing other odd sounds, including footsteps and what sounded like things being shuffled around. I knew it was pointless to go downstairs to try to catch whatever was making the disturbance because it would stop as soon as I made a move. I tried my best to get some sleep despite all the activity, and I thought about the fact that I was going to need to keep my guard up as the investigation continued.

The next morning over breakfast, we discussed the events that had happened so far. Dave wanted to do some sessions in the cabin, but I decided to take a walk out to the woods and check out the activity there.

It was humid, but still a nice day. I walked over to the path that led into the forest and continued into the trees. It was a massive area, and I knew that I'd need to be careful and pay attention to the markers so I wouldn't get lost.

I started up a ghost box, and right away, I started getting references to soldiers. This was no surprise; there had been a number of battles and skirmishes fought on the land during the Civil War. There's no telling how many soldiers were fatally wounded and lost their lives on the land. The communication was sporadic, and there were references to bloodshed, death, and fighting.

Something led me to continue walking, and I found myself led to the back of the brick rancher, and right behind the window where the little girl had been pulled out. A response came through the ghost box that referenced rape and murder. The thing is, I never got a sense of the little girl's spirit or presence. Usually, I get a message if there is a spirit present that wants or needs help. This isn't always definite; there can always be something blocking communication, or the spirit itself could be holding back, but either way, I didn't feel there was anyone there who needed or wanted my help. The story is, of course, disturbing, and I could only hope that if it were true, the little girl had already found peace.

I headed back over to the main cabin and decided to check out the back room. I carried in an SLS camera. This camera uses light sensors to detect alleged spirits and displays them on screen in the form of stick figures.

I had a ghost box running at the same time, and I was getting very sexual references coming through. Dennis had previously captured a video of a strange light anomaly in this room. Right away, stick figures showed up on the SLS camera display. They seemed to be interacting with each other. The two figures got close to each other, and it started to look like there was a sexual interaction going on. I was taken aback by the display, never having seen something like it show up on the SLS. It was intriguing, though, when considering the stories that the location had once been a brothel.

Was its residual energy in the room, or were there spirits still present going through the motions? I shook my head, thinking how crazy it was that there was such a wide variety of activity going on at the property.

The day had gone by fast, and it was getting dark. I regrouped with Dave, and we decided to go outside back to the forest area I had investigated previously. We took some equipment and headed down the path into the woods. It was pretty dark, and right away, we were getting activity. The ghost box was giving references to soldiers and combat, just like I had received when I investigated earlier that day. There were strange sounds around us, and I knew it wasn't just animals, but something else.

We ended up on a main path adjacent to the forest with a number of different paths that connected to it. As we were walking, we heard the distinct sound of a horse trotting towards us. We stopped and listened to the sound. Again, there was the feeling of being watched, and now, with the sound of a horse approaching, we really felt like someone was coming towards us!

A phantom horse was heard near the Cabin on 360.

Watching the road and the area around us, we continued walking down the path. We both saw a shadow quickly dart across the road in front of us. Was it the spirit of a soldier? References to soldiers and battles continued to come in over the ghost box, and the sound of the horse faded away. Clearly, there was a lot of residual energy at this location. I had a strong sense of the soldiers who had lost their lives on the land. It was fascinating, but tragic at the same time.

We headed back to our base at the cabin to take a quick break and decided on our next move. I still couldn't completely shake the experience of something crawling up my neck. The thought of those massive spiders creeping around the basement was in the back of my head, but I had to wonder if there was something demonic at the property. We decided to go to the brick rancher and do some investigating. As I've stated, walking through the doors of the brick house, there was an instant feeling of heavy, oppressive energy. It was so substantial that the feeling is very hard to put into words. I really wanted to get to the bottom of this and figure out what was haunting the building.

Soon we were back in the damn basement again. I thought about the spiders, but overall, I felt more prepared this time. I knew something had tried to use my fear of spiders to intimidate me and cause me to be vulnerable, but I wasn't about to let it get to me spiritually. I said a quick prayer of protection to further empower me.

Standing there in the dark basement, the ghost box was blaring, and I was trying to use all of my senses to determine what was there. I took out the SLS camera, hoping to catch an image of the thing.

The spirit box was giving lots of dark, malevolent types of responses. Something yelled out very loudly over the box, and it suddenly shut off. Dave picked up the box and tried to determine why it shut down, but he couldn't find an answer. We turned the box back on, and now it seemed as if the energy in the room was changing. It wasn't a good feeling.

I started panning around the basement with the SLS camera. Never in a million years did I expect what happened next. As I panned around the room, the camera hit an area to the left of the stairs. On the screen, starting to take shape, was some kind of anomaly. It was moving along, then hit the floor, and started scrambling around. It wasn't a typical stick figure, and I was puzzled by what the manifestation was and exactly what was forming. For several seconds, the figure shifted around and came together as it formed fully. I felt the hair go up on the back of my neck, and there was a funny feeling in the pit of my stomach, warning signs that something was going on for sure. I screamed out loud, "Get the hell out of here. No f*#@ing way. It looks like a f*#@ing spider!"

Sure enough, the shifting image on the SLS screen had formed into the shape of a spider. There was a live stream going during this incident, and the people watching were as shocked as I was. I suddenly realized that the spot on the stairs where the figure had started to form was the exact spot where Dennis had killed the huge spider the night before when we were all in the basement.

In some ways, it was a sickening feeling. I had the strong sense that whatever kind of entity was down in the basement was again trying to use my fear of spiders to come after me. As this was happening, I felt something on my neck near my ear. Once again, it was a phantom touch on the same area of my neck that had been touched before.

We didn't do much more that night. After the experience, I felt very drained of energy. I thought a lot about the feelings in that place and the evidence that had been collected. I truly believed that something, something very dark, was using my fear of spiders against me. No human entity would do this or be able to do this, only something demonic. It had targeted me for some reason, maybe because of the work I do as a demonologist, helping people and doing my best to rescue souls and help them cross over to God.

The next day, Dave packed up his gear and headed home. Despite all the intensity, I wasn't quite ready to leave. I decided to call Judy, a friend of mine who lives close to the cabin. Judy is a sensitive, and I wanted to see what she could pick up at the location. Luckily, she was available and came over to meet up with Dennis and me before I had to leave.

The main cabin

Judy did a walk-through of the buildings and was able to confirm some of the same sensations that I had picked up on while investigating the site. The place also left a mark on her so to speak. I'll let her tell it in her own words:

"My friend, Sean, was investigating a place called The

Cabin on 360, and he invited me to come see him there. I had never heard of this place, and Sean didn't tell me anything about it. I have psychic abilities like Sean, and he said he wanted me to do a walk-through of a house on the property to see what psychic impression I could get. We walked into the living room of the brick ranch house. There was definitely heavy energy there. I was quickly drawn to the first bedroom. It was so light and peaceful in that room. It was so different than the rest of the house. In the very next room, I felt intense anger and mental anguish. It was at that point that Sean informed me that the young girl who slept in the first room was murdered by her stepbrother who slept in the second room. Sean then led me to the basement and wow, it was difficult to breathe. The basement had cement columns, and I told Sean I kept seeing a dark shadow hiding behind one of the columns. We had only been in the basement a few minutes when I suddenly felt a spirit go through my body. It had gotten difficult for us both to breathe, so we left the house and went back to the cabin.

"Dennis asked me what I thought of the house. I told him how heavy the whole house felt except the first bedroom that was so light and peaceful. Dennis told me he did a blessing and cleansing of that room to help the murdered girl find peace. I do believe she's at peace. Sean told me he believed the same thing after having been there two days investigating.

"The next day, when I woke up, I noticed I had bruises on my arms and legs. These bruises were not there before, and I had not gotten hurt. I immediately called Sean and told him about the bruises. I told him I thought it was from the spirit in the basement that had passed through me. He thought it was as well."

It had been an intense two days investigating the Cabin on 360. I was still in shock about the spider manifestation as I packed up and headed home. Ryan and Dennis told me that no one had ever experienced anything close to that in the basement or anywhere else on the property.

I told Ryan and Dennis that their location was a trifecta of paranormal energy. It's ironic the place is called the Cabin on 360 because when there's paranormal energy, it comes at you from all directions.

It was a five-hour drive back home, and I was beyond exhausted on every level. Sometimes, investigations like this one create a "paranormal hangover." This was usually due to the combination of having to deal with so many energies, having to stay on guard spiritually, and spending long hours actively investigating. Areas that have high levels of negative energy and history are often even more difficult to deal with, creating a whole other level of exhaustion. It's important to realize and remember that on paranormal investigations, spirits don't just drain energy from electronic devices, but from the humans who are spending time at the site.

When I got home, I was still exhausted, even more so after having to make the drive. I grabbed a quick shower and got ready for bed. Just as I was about to climb in and get some sleep, I saw a huge spider drop down in front of me to the middle of my bed! I couldn't help but scream out. I grabbed a towel, got the spider in it, and threw the thing out of the window. I said out loud, "Are you serious?"

After everything that had happened in Virginia, was this thing still coming after me, still using my fear of spiders to mess with me? After I calmed down, I was finally able to get some much-needed rest.

A few days later, I received a call from Dave. He had been going through footage from the investigation at the cabin. He told me about something captured on video while I was running the SLS camera.

When the spider thing was forming, a ball of energy came down from the ceiling and floated over my head for a few seconds before rising back up through the ceiling. This was right when I felt something touching my neck and ear. This was further confirmation of my experience and the fact that I was picking up on something around me in the basement.

I've never investigated a place where something tried so hard to use a particular fear against me in its manifestation. It was crazy.

Three weeks later, I was going about my regular day when

I got a call from Ryan. He quickly said, "You won't believe what we just discovered down in the basement, and I don't think you're gonna like it."

Ryan sent me a photo. It was the biggest spider I had ever seen. The thing was a wolf spider, and I swear it was the size of a dinner plate. I almost lost it when I saw the photo. So creepy. What was it with these spiders and that basement?

Ryan told me that Dennis had knocked the thing down, and it was so big that he heard it when it hit the floor. He sprayed it with a chemical spray, hoping to kill it, and left it where it was. He went back later and discovered that half of the thing's body was gone as if part of it had gotten up and walked away!

The whole story was the thing of nightmares. Again, Ryan said they had never seen a spider like that on the property, not until I had been there, and we saw that first one on the wall. Was it the demonic entity doing this just to taunt me, to reach out indirectly, and say, "See what I can do?"

I look forward to returning again to the Cabin on 360, but I'm not looking forward to that basement and the damn spiders. I'm thinking that on my next trip, I'll take a hazmat suit and carry a blowtorch. Spiders. No, thank you.

One of the dreadful spiders at the 360 Cabin

BORG'S
WOODS
NATURE
PRESERVE
BERGEN COUNTY
DEPARTMENT
OF PARKS
GREEN ACRES
LOCAL ASSISTANCE PROGRAM
THIS SITE DEDICATED TO

Woods Where Evil Lurks

Borg's Woods is a nature preserve in Bergen County, New Jersey. The preserve is just over fourteen acres of woodlands and wetlands in the towns of Hackensack and Maywood. The preserve is part of the Bergen County park system. It's in kind of a weird spot, surrounded by residential developments.

The forest was almost cut down for condos in the 1980s when the land was owned by Macromedia, Inc., but people fought the plan. The Borg's Woods Preservation Coalition, which was active between 1986 and 1995, also prevented a townhouse project from taking part of the woods. It was Republican State Senator, Pat Schuber, who finally helped preserve the area. The land was finally purchased by Bergen County, and the area became the preserve it is today.

I had never heard of these woods before, but always being on the lookout and keeping my ears open for paranormal stories, I started hearing strange things about the woods. I got a call from two friends of mine, Amy and Christy, who started telling me about what they had learned from a friend about the woods.

Reportedly, the woods had been the location of satanic activity in the 1950s, and there were stories of ritual murders there. My interest was certainly piqued by the stories, and I was anxious to check out the location.

One night, the three of us decided to go to the woods and see what we could find. When we arrived, it was nighttime, and the woods were very dark. We headed down a path and deep into the woods. We had no idea what to expect or what we would find, but the feeling was certainly ominous. The deeper into the woods we went, the stronger the feeling became. You might think this has to do with the fact that we were exploring in the deep woods, but there was something more, something hard to describe.

At one point, we discovered a hut of some kind in the woods. It looked like it had been made of broken tree branches. I wondered if it was made by someone, or a group of people, for shelter, but it was hard to tell. When we walked up to the hut, the ominous feeling turned even more unsettling. I felt a heavy pressure on my chest, and what I sensed was a dark presence. As we stood there looking around, we all felt like we were being watched.

As if the pressure on my chest and the feeling of being watched wasn't enough, we started seeing a shadow figure darting around us. Now, mind you, it was pitch black where we were, but this thing, whatever it was, was a shadow that was even darker than the night's natural darkness. To make this even creepier, this shadow figure started circling us!

I turned on a spirit box to see if there were any spirits who would communicate. I started asking questions and right away, there were nasty, dark voices coming through in response. The guttural voices spat out satanic and demonic references. "We are Legion," said a deep voice.

As a demonologist, it was a phrase I was certainly familiar with. Legion, the demons of Gadarenes, is the name given in the New Testament. It involved Jesus' exorcism of the entities, and they are notable as the only named demons in the New Testament.

The story involves Jesus' encounter with a man possessed by demons. The book of Mark chronicles the encounter, starting with a verse about the power of a demon-possessed man:

"This man lived in the tombs, and no one could bind him anymore, not even with a chain. For he had often been chained hand and foot, but he tore the chains apart and broke the irons on his feet. No one was strong enough to subdue him. Night and day among the tombs and in the hills, he would cry out and cut himself with stones" (Mark 5: 3-5).

When the man saw Jesus, he was terrified, and Jesus addressed the entity that had taken the man over.

"For Jesus had said to him, 'Come out of this man, you impure spirit!'

Then Jesus asked him, 'What is your name?'

'My name is Legion,' he replied, 'for we are many.'"

(Mark 5: 8-9).

The reference to Legion, spit out with such a nasty voice over the spirit box, gave me a strong feeling of anxiety. It was clearly a negative force trying to project evil intentions towards us. The feeling was all the stronger since we were deep in the woods near a weird hut that someone had built. At this point, one of the girls started feeling a burning sensation on her leg. I knew it was a sign of a possible attack and was concerned that something serious was starting to unfold. I went over and checked her leg. Sure enough, there were these long, red scratches running up her leg.

I knew it was time to clear out. We had seen enough for this trip, and I knew that I would be returning to investigate the location further.

On my second trip to Borg's Woods, Amy and Christy were both with me again. We also had another member in the party this time around, Amy's boyfriend, Eric. Eric is a great guy and to this day remains a good friend of mine. We have investigated many locations together.

We made our way down the same path as before and found the odd man-made hut again. I quickly found that it was just like the first time there. The anxiety returned, the feeling that something was watching from out of the darkness, the general creepy energy of the place.

We turned on a spirit box and sure enough, negative responses started to come through. As I listened to the nasty, guttural voices come through again, I thought about the previous time at the spot and the mention of the demonic legion.

Just then, both of the girls heard what they said sounded like the snort of a pig. We all noticed a terrible, strong odor that smelled like urine. Amy, who had been scratched on the previous visit, started to act strange and was spacing out.

Again, I started thinking about Jesus' encounter and his casting out of the demons. In the story, after commanding the man, or rather, the entities controlling the man, to reveal its identity, the demons showed fear of what was coming.

"And he begged Jesus again and again not to send them out of the area. A large heard of pigs was feeding on the nearby hillside. The demons begged Jesus, 'Send us among the pigs; allow us to go into them.' He gave them permission, and the impure spirits came out and went into the pigs. The herd, about two thousand in number, rushed down the steep bank into the lake and were drowned" (Mark 5: 10-13).

What was this convergence of things happening out in the woods? Amy was so spaced out that she didn't even look present. We tried to snap her out of it, and she finally responded, saying she couldn't feel half of her body, and that she felt like she had lost consciousness for a few minutes.

I was getting very concerned for everyone's safety. The spirit box was still running, and a loud male voiced growled out loudly, "They're gonna get sick!"

The voice was forceful and, as it came through the box, both of the girls started to puke. Eric and I looked at each other in shock, wondering how the hell this was possible. Did this thing have that much energy that it could make two human beings sick like that by projecting its energy?

The two girls kept throwing up, and I knew we needed to get them out of the woods as quickly as possible. We started down the path, headed for the parking spot. The whole way, walking down the path, the girls kept stopping and throwing up over and over.

We made it back to my car. I grabbed a bottle of holy water and immediately put some on their foreheads. Right after this, they stopped vomiting. We left after this, now knowing, without a doubt, that something very evil was making its home in Borg's Woods.

I later learned just how angry Eric was after seeing what had happened to Amy. He made a return to the site alone on another day and threw holy water all over everything in the area around the weird hut. The whole time he was flinging the holy water, he was telling the thing to back off and go back where it belonged.

He told me what he had done, and I was concerned. Bringing personal emotions into such a situation can be very dangerous. Demonic forces can easily twist emotions and intentions and use them against you. Additionally, an emotional state can cause cracks in your spiritual protection and create an opening for negative entities to get in. Demonic forces will use any opening they can, and they will definitely take advantage of emotional states.

Deep in Borg's Woods

I didn't talk to Eric or either of the girls for a few weeks, but the next time I did, I learned that Amy had been having a recurring nightmare. She told me about the dream, one that was creepy, to say the least.

She told me she kept dreaming that we were back in the woods and that something in the darkness was after us. This thing would reach out from the shadows, grab us by the legs, and pull us away into the darkness. We all would get taken except her. Amy was left standing there, hearing us scream to her for help. Left alone in the dark woods, Amy would watch as a tiny little pig came walking up to her. At first, it was friendly, but it would suddenly turn vicious and attack her. She would wake up in a sweat.

The same dream was recurring over and over. Amy couldn't understand what it meant or why it was happening to her, but she was very disturbed by it.

After the incidents, Eric started digging a bit more for information about the woods. He learned that a few years prior, a friend of his had been in the woods with a small group of people. They were chased out by a large shadow figure in the shape of a horse.

There were other stories, too. Reportedly, local police had found signs of animal sacrifices having been done in the area. There appeared to be evidence of Santeria rituals having been done in the woods, and there were other occult things, too. Someone had, evidently, been using a Ouija board in Borg's Woods. I had to wonder, what were they trying to contact out there, or what had they conjured?

On top of all of this, there were rumors that mob hits had been carried out in the woods and that some of the victims could be buried there. Any of these factors could cause dark entities to be in the woods, but if there were a combination of these elements, it could make things even more intense.

During all of this, I had a vision of a black mist hovering over Eric in his home. My first thought was that it had something to do with Borg's Woods. Had he angered something evil by trying to command it to leave its spot?

Since Amy and Eric were both part of the Borg's Woods incidents, I have asked them both to share their experiences. Amy writes:

"Borg's will always be a place that sticks with me. From what I remember of that night, it was not something I can fully explain. I remember there were a few of us there, and we were all standing around the "hut" we always stood by, and questions were being asked to the spirit box. I remember starting to feel a bit weird but just brushed it off. Eventually, the weird feeling turned into a nauseous feeling, and then the nauseous feeling turned to throwing up. I had no control over it. I felt like I got punched in the gut and that had me throwing up.

"One other person with us was having a very similar thing happening at the same time. The feeling did not go away. We also heard what sounded like pig noises coming from the trees around us.

"Whatever is in those woods has stuck with me since I was there. I have had dreams, weird dreams, since we left. One dream (a dream that began that night), that I still have to this day, has this weird creature with red eyes creeping around the upstairs of the house I used to live in. I am watching him as he is watching me in my bed. It has been almost two years since I lived in that house, yet I still have that dream.

"Occasionally, the red-eyed creature will resemble a really big pig, but sometimes it is just a creature that I can't really make out. It always had red eyes.

"I also have a dream that links Borg's and the Hinsdale house for some reason. The Hinsdale house is another haunted location in upstate New York that some of us have been to. It has a dark past.

"In the dream, I am in Borg's woods alone, and I can hear all of my friends screaming for help. I start to run towards the screams, but I just keep running and running and don't seem to get anywhere. Finally, I break out of the woods, and somehow, I am at the Hinsdale house. I get to the door, and an old lady opens her mouth to scream, but the screams of a pig come out. I always wake up at that moment."

Hearing about Amy's nightmares, I was again reminded of Jesus casting demons out and into the swine. There was certainly a lot of pig symbology that kept coming up in relation to Borg's Woods. For me, this again confirmed that something demonic was at work in the New Jersey forest.

Over time, Eric and I investigated the woods many times. Living close to the area, Eric was able to learn a lot about the place from locals. Like Amy and I, he was deeply affected by the time spent at the site. As he writes:

"Sean and I have been investigating the haunted Borg's Woods for over two years. Growing up close by the woods in New Jersey, I remember hearing ghost stories about the place from the time when I was a kid. I remember hearing stories of satanic rituals being performed and stories of people using Ouija boards there.

"When I was in high school, I remember a teacher telling me that a cop had found a decapitated head in the woods.

"Two friends of mine had witnessed a horse-like entity that chased them out of the woods.

"Over the past couple of years of investigating the place, we've come into contact with something I believe to be demonic in nature. The first night, I went with Sean and two friends. At one point during the investigation, a voice came through the spirit box saying, "Gonna make them sick." Both girls hunched over and started vomiting, and one went into a trance-like state. We walked the girls out of there, and Sean blessed them with holy water and recited some prayers. The intense evening left an impression on me. Being of the Catholic faith, I was seriously affected by this and chose to go back alone.

"I gathered video and audio evidence of something evil there. I said prayers and threw holy water around the area. I asked if there was a demonic entity in the woods, and a voice came through my spirit box that said, "Satan!"

"I believe an entity followed me home and tried to get at me. The thing has scratched me on my neck and has tried to make me angry. My bed also shook, and words were put into my head telepathically, a voice that said, "Blood."

During the course of our time investigating the haunted woods, Eric and I met a local girl named Christine. It turned out that Christine lived right across from Borg's Woods when she was growing up. She'd had a lot of strange experiences connected to the woods, herself, and it was interesting talking to her and hearing about her experiences. Hearing Christine's stories further confirmed for me that there have been a lot of dark events in the woods that have been hushed up by those involved and by those who simply didn't want the stories to get out. I can understand why people wouldn't want to discuss such things. As I stated, Borg's Woods is surrounded by residential neighborhoods. People walk through the park, take their children and their dogs there, and generally try to enjoy the natural elements. But when night falls, it's a different place.

Places like this are often used by undesirables for illegal activities. Some of it is typical teenage ignorance, drug use, playing around with satanic books and rituals, and so forth, but some of it is much more serious. People who practice Santeria and related traditions often go to places like Borg's Woods to conduct their animal sacrifices. Adults who practice witchcraft and satanic traditions also like to use locations like this one for their ceremonies. These factors and others can create dark portals of energy in the land.

Christine told me about growing up near the woods and some of her experiences related to the place:

"Ever since I was a little girl, I was told never to go into the Borg's Woods Nature Preserve alone because there are 'not good people in those woods.' Every now and then, I would hear things and see shadow type beings, but I would make myself believe that it was an animal or kids causing trouble and continue on with my day because I did not want to believe I lived next to an evil place.

"I never had good feelings about those woods. They always gave off a bad vibe, and I was always hesitant to go near them. I am an empath, so I feel things very strongly. I can read a room very well, and my gut instinct is usually right.

"My first experience with Borg's happened when I was

in my early twenties. I remember it was early April. It was warm out, and the woods looked beautiful, so I decided to walk through them. I got this weird feeling in the pit of my stomach, like the feeling when you are incredibly disappointed in someone. I shook those feelings off because I figured it is daylight, what is the worst that can happen?

"I was walking along the path when I saw a woman out of the corner of my eye; she was audibly crying. The woman was in an all-white dress, and she looked extremely sad. I stopped and turned around, thinking how oddly dressed the woman was and to ask if she was okay. It is not every day you see a woman crying in the woods wearing a white dress. I turned around, and she was gone.

"Not thinking anything of it, I kept walking. I got to the pond in the woods, and I saw her again. She had dark jet-black hair and pale skin, and she just stared at me with her sad eyes. She did not move; she did not speak; she just stood there. I turned right around and left. I wanted to stay, but my body said I had to go. For several months after the sighting, I was intrigued. I looked up everything about the woods and really could not find much about what happened there.

"To this day, when I drive past the woods, I often see her out of the corner of my eye, standing there as if inviting me back in."

Christine's story about the lady in white was fascinating. Who was this spirit? I thought about the potential that it was the ghost of one of the purported mob victims, crying out for help or trying to make contact with someone. As interesting as it was, there was another story from Christine that was more chilling because of its connections to my own investigations.

"One September afternoon, I wanted to go for a run through the woods. I decided to go back later in the day around three or four in the afternoon. When I entered the woods this time, there was a different feeling about the place. Instead of the sad feelings I got before, there was a feeling of dread and fear. My body was telling me to run away. The entire time I was in the woods, I felt like someone was watching me. I kept on running but was nervous about the eyes I felt glaring down on my back. I turned around, but there was nothing there."

What hides deep in Borg's Woods?

"I stopped to catch my breath by an old creepy looking tree with a hole in it. I thought to myself what a strange tree; I never really noticed it before. As I examined the tree, I thought I heard a whisper of my name, and then someone touched my shoulder. I got nervous and turned around, but there was no one there. I kept on walking and heard footsteps behind me. I started to walk a little faster this time, hoping to get out of the woods before whatever was behind me caught up.

"I had a weird feeling again, and I stopped for some odd reason. I turned around, and I saw a shadow figure behind me. It was tall, and it looked like the figure of a large man. Whatever it was, it was horrifying. I began to run, but it caught up right before I could exit the woods. It pushed me to the ground. I don't even remember getting up and leaving.

"After that experience, I have been back in the woods, and I still see him. He loves to hang out by the tree or by this creepy fort or hut in the back of the woods. He enjoys taunting me from the edge of the forest when I drive by. He is not alone in there; he has many evil spirit friends who love to torture the living. That night, and to this very day, I have dreams about the shadow man. He comes in two forms, one as a man completely in black and one as a man with a pig's head."

The pig entity of Borg's Woods

There it was again, a pig reference. My mind raced back to the story of Jesus casting out the demons into swine and all the strange pig-related manifestations that connected to Borg's Woods.

I learned that Amy and Christy had gone to the woods on another occasion. They went out to the creepy hut and actually played with a Ouija board.

Obviously, this is not something I would ever have done myself. I, personally, believe Ouija boards are dangerous, and that they can make things worse in a place like Borg's. That seemed to be the case this time around.

The day after they used the board, Christy started to have some weird things go on inside her house. She didn't feel right and believed that something was trying to oppress her.

She had a dream about some sort of demonic creature that came in the form of a horse and talked to her. She couldn't make out what the thing was saying, but it gave her its name—Gamigin.

Was this the same entity that had manifested in front of Eric's friends in the shape of a horse shadow figure? I decided to do some research into the name Christy had gotten.

Gamigin is a fallen angel and one of the 72 spirits of Solomon. In Hell, Gamigin is a duke commanding thirty legions of demons. He appears in the form of a small horse or ass and can change into human form. Gamigin can summon the souls of drowned men and those who are in purgatory.

This demon is mentioned in a famous magical book, *"The Goetia: The Lesser Key of Solomon the King,"* written by S.L. MacGregor Mathers in 1904. The book calls the demon by two different names, Samigina and Gamigin.

This book has been used to summon and control demons using ritual magic. Obviously, this is not a practice that I condone, but the books are useful as a reference for information on various named demonic entities.

I found similar references to the demon in another, older text, the *"Pseudomonarchia Daemonum,"* or *"False Monarchy of*

Demons." The book was written long before *"The Lesser Key of Solomon"* and has some differences, although it was later incorporated into the Solomon book for use in summoning demons.

Researching this stuff is always like digging deeply into a dark rabbit hole. One piece of information leads to another, and so many things connect together, making you wonder what the meaning of it all is.

On another occasion, Christy woke up and couldn't breathe. She was shocked to find that her bedsheets were wrapped around her neck and double knotted. It seemed impossible that something like this could happen just by her moving around in her sleep.

I was very concerned about the incident, and Eric and I went over right away and blessed her house.

Since first investigating in Borg's Woods, references to the site have turned up around both Eric and I on occasion. It's hard to say what originally caused such dark entities to take up their home in the woods. With so many rumors and stories involving the place, it becomes difficult to sort out.

If anyone chooses to take a walk in this forest, best use a lot of caution, and be on guard, there are dark things lurking there.

Woods Where Evil Lurks

OCEAN AV

The Amityville Resurgence

On November 13, 1974, one of the most gruesome crimes in New York history occurred. On that fateful date, Ronald DeFeo, Jr. shot and killed six members of his own family in their suburban Long Island home at 112 Ocean Avenue.

The 23-year-old DeFeo used a high-powered rifle to kill his parents, Ronald, Sr., 43 and Louise, 42, his sisters Dawn, 18 and Allison, 13, and his brothers Marc, 12 and John Matthew, 7. Later investigations showed that DeFeo's parents had both been shot twice while the children were each shot once. The murder weapon was a .35 caliber lever action Marlin 336C rifle.

The killer had crept around the house committing the murders at 3:15 a.m., a time that would later prove significant in the strange stories that arose about the Amityville house.

At 6:30 in the evening, Ronald DeFeo, Jr. ran into Henry's Bar and shouted, "You've got to help me! I think my mother and father are shot!" DeFeo led a small group of bar patrons back to the family home where they discovered the murders. One man in the group, Joe Yeswit, called Suffolk County Police who arrived on the scene and discovered a total of six people dead. Bizarrely, all of the victims were murdered while lying face down in their beds. They were all in their nightclothes, and it was believed they had each been killed in their sleep.

Ronald, Jr., also known as "Butch," was taken to the police station, not under suspicion, but for his own protection. The man had suggested to police officers that the killings had been carried about by a mob hitman. Once at the police station, officers began to notice inconsistencies in DeFeo's claims, and the Mafia tale quickly unraveled.

The following day, Ronald DeFeo, Jr. confessed to killing his parents and siblings. DeFeo was tried and convicted the following year on November 21. He was found guilty of six counts of 2nd-degree murder. Judge Thomas Stark announced the sentence on December 4—six concurrent sentences of 25 to life for the horrible murders of the DeFeo adults and children.

Ronald DeFeo, Jr. was an avid drug user, shooting heroin and using LSD. His lawyer used an insanity defense in an effort to get the young man off. DeFeo's story changed on numerous occasions, but one of his key claims was that he "heard voices" that were plotting against him.

Despite the insanity plea from a clearly unbalanced person, Dr. Harold Zolan, a witness for the prosecution, testified that DeFeo was aware of his actions when he carried out the murders.

DeFeo is currently held at the Sullivan Correctional Facility in Fallsburg, New York.

Over the years, Ronald, Jr. has told a lot of stories about the murders, including a claim that once he started shooting, he couldn't stop himself. DeFeo said the voices in his head told him to kill his family. At another point, he claimed a hooded figure handed him the rifle that he used in the murders.

Investigators were puzzled by some of the details in the case. Why had no one in the neighborhood heard the gunshots? Why was every victim lying face down in their beds? And perhaps most oddly, why did none of the victims hear the gunshots and attempt to escape? No sedatives were found in the victims' bodies, leading some to speculate that DeFeo had an accomplice.

The saga of the DeFeo murders, as tragic as it was, may have ended with Ronald, Jr.'s sentencing, but there was more to come.

In December 1975, thirteen months after the murders, George and Kathleen Lutz purchased the DeFeo home for what they believed was the bargain price of $80,000. The Dutch Colonial style home had lots of appeal with its stylish exterior, swimming pool, a boathouse, and five bedrooms.

The Lutz family included George and his wife Kathy, along with three children from Kathy's previous marriage: Daniel, Christopher, and Melissa or "Missy." The family also had a dog in-tow, a Labrador named Harry.

The relator told George and Kathy about the murders, but the house was such a dream buy that they decided they could ignore the home's past. There was something else the Lutz family ignored—most of the DeFeo family's furniture was still in the house. Rather than buy new furniture for their home, the Lutz family considered it a bonus and kept the furnishings. From a paranormal perspective, this is another bad idea. Considering the murders and other emotional events that took place in the home, the house itself, and the furnishings, could all hold energy from the tragedy. Additionally, leaving the house the way it was during the deaths could have been a trigger for the activity that was to come during the time the Lutz family was in the home.

The events that followed have been written about extensively, fictionalized, and portrayed in books and on the silver screen numerous times. I won't recount all of the events here, but there are a number of things that stand out to me:

Although he was not a Catholic, George wanted to have the house blessed. Kathy was a non-practicing Catholic, so neither knew much about the process. Nevertheless, they arranged to have a priest come to the home. The priest, Father Mancuso, claimed he heard a voice tell him to "Get Out," after which he felt a slap across his face. Mancuso later developed a high fever and strange blisters on his hands that resembled stigmata, the manifestation of the wounds of Christ.

Kathy began having vivid nightmares connected to the murders. She soon realized that her dreams showed her the order of the deaths, taking her through the terrible night step by step.

As for George, he began waking up every night at 3:15 a.m. He would arise from bed and go to the boathouse to check on things. Lutz would later learn that he was waking each night at the time the murders occurred.

The children all started sleeping on their stomachs, lying in bed in the same manner as the DeFeo victims were found dead.

During George's wanderings around the property, he discovered a hidden room in the basement behind a set of shelves. The room was not shown on the home's blueprints. Dubbed "the red room," the family dog wouldn't go near the spot, and in fact, wouldn't go in the basement at all.

Missy started talking about her imaginary friend, "Jodie." According to the Lutz's, Jodie wasn't just an imaginary entity. George reported that in the early morning hours of Christmas Day 1975, he found himself in the boathouse looking up at the house. He saw Missy in her bedroom window. Behind her was a demonic pig-like creature with red glowing eyes. George rushed inside and up to the girl's room. He found her passed out in bed and a rocking chair in the room, slowly rocking back and forth as if someone was sitting in it.

Kathy had a sighting of the bizarre pig figure, too. Her daughter told her; Jodie had climbed out of the window. Kathy saw the creature's glowing red eyes. The Lutz' also claimed they discovered hoof prints in the snow on New Year's Day in 1976.

Other strange things were occurring in the Amityville house. The front door started slamming when no one was around. George would run to the door, hoping to catch someone, but each time nothing was there. A crucifix hanging in the home kept getting turned upside-down. Flies started swarming the house, even though the weather was cold. This is often a sign of demonic activity. One of the most well-known stories involved slime oozing from the walls.

As things progressed in the home, George started to realize that he bore a significant resemblance to Ronald DeFeo, Jr. He even started going to the same bar that DeFeo had frequented.

Realizing that something was terribly wrong in their home, George and Kathy decided to recite prayers. George claimed that during the prayers, he heard voices in his head telling him to stop.

On January 14, 1976, after a total of twenty-eight days in the home, George, Kathy, their three children, and their dog fled the house leaving behind all their possessions. A mover later went into the home and retrieved the family's belongings. The mover reported no paranormal activity from his time in the house.

Horror writer, Jay Anson, turned the Lutz's experiences into a bestselling novel, "The Amityville Horror," launching a legendary haunted house story. The book was published in 1977 and turned into a hit film in 1979.

The Amityville case has long been controversial. Rumors of hoaxes, false accounts, and outright fabrication have been a part of the story since the start. Some people believe the entire tale is false and that the story was made up for financial gain.

Sadly, this is often the case with paranormal events. Speculations and questions arise, especially when the media gets involved. I know from firsthand experience that sometimes it is about the money. But I also know there are plenty of times that families really need help because they're dealing with a serious and unexplainable situation.

While many people doubt the Lutz family's story, there are things that indicate they did experience things in the home. George took polygraph tests conducted by two of the nation's top five polygraph experts. The results indicated he was not lying.

While we can only speculate, I, personally, believe the Lutz family experienced some profound paranormal events in the home during their time there. One thing is for sure, Ronald DeFeo, Jr. committed a horrible series of murders in the house, and his brutal actions left some kind of impression. Whether you believe the story or not, it became one of the most well-known haunted house stories of our time. Even today, if you mention "The Amityville House," people will know something about the story.

Living close to the Amityville home for many years, and having such a deep interest in the paranormal, I have always been interested in stories and information about the place. I always wondered how much of the story was true and if the reported demonic activity was as bad as the movies portrayed.

I had heard claims that the DeFeo family experienced paranormal events when they were living in the house. Reportedly, Ronald, Sr. put religious items all around the home, possibly in an effort to evoke spiritual protections.

There were also claims that the home had been built on Native American burial grounds. This is a frequent claim about haunted locations, so much so that it almost becomes a joke. In this particular case, it is interesting to note that in some traditions, burying someone face down is a sign of disrespect. Recalling that the entire DeFeo family died face down, was something showing its disrespect for them? Considering the strange circumstances around the murders and the reported paranormal events that took place afterwards, it's important to look at all the possibilities.

I've often wondered why all these people laid still in their beds, not waking up to the sound of gunfire, not trying to run away as their family members were killed. Why were they all in the same position? To me, it's as if there was some sort of mass induced sleep paralysis that was projected onto the entire family, a condition that allowed Ronald to go around the home and kill each of the people one by one.

Let's also recall that no one in the neighborhood reported hearing the gunshots. Even the police were puzzled by this, and during interviews with locals, they discovered that the only noise people recalled was the sound of a dog barking.

Did some malevolent force muffle the gunshots? There is such a sense of evil around the events of that terrible night; that to me, it feels like a perfect storm of darkness.

These thoughts and questions have been on my mind since I first started researching the Amityville case. Trying to follow all of the various pieces of the DeFeo and Lutz story isn't easy. Once I started looking at the paranormal aspects of the case, two names came up immediately, Ed and Lorraine Warren.

The Warrens were pioneers of the paranormal field. They got involved with the Amityville case in 1976 when they investigated the haunting. During an investigation in the home by the Warrens, one of the world's most famous ghost photos was captured. During the 1976 investigation, team member and professional photographer, Gene Campbell, set up an automatic camera to take infrared pictures on the home's second-floor landing. The black and white film captured a creepy image that has haunted people for years. The photo shows a portion of the stairs and the open doors of two rooms. Peering out of one of the rooms, and looking over the stair rail, is the face of a young boy. His eyes are solid white and appear to glow somewhat. The boy bears a resemblance to young John Matthew DeFeo, one of the children murdered in the home.

George Lutz revealed the photograph in 1979 during an appearance on the Merv Griffin Show. Skeptics, of course, don't believe the picture shows a ghost, but despite their cries, the photo has never been debunked and remains one of the most puzzling paranormal photographs in history.

Lorraine Warren, a psychic, said she felt uncomfortable in the Amityville house. So much so that she claimed there was a "personification of evil" at the location. The Warrens also claimed they were attacked when they went in the home and they contacted clergy for additional spiritual help.

Lorraine would later state that the Amityville house affected her and Ed's personal lives more than any other case they worked on during their fifty years of paranormal research.

Ed was a religious demonologist, and the couple had been involved in various cases of hauntings and dark supernatural events, but something from the Amityville case followed and plagued them.

The Warrens claimed that not only was Ronald, Jr. actively using drugs but that he was also practicing the occult. Specifically, Ronald, Jr. was reportedly delving into satanic witchcraft and was using the mysterious red room in the home's basement for rituals.

Ed Warren believed that DeFeo's practices, coupled with his hatred for his own father, created spiritual vulnerabilities, making the young man open for attachment and possession by evil entities.

The Warrens talked to Father Mancuso, who told them about his personal encounters in the home when trying to bless the house for the Lutz family.

After they visited the Amityville house, the Warrens claimed they had personal encounters in their own home that night. Lorraine said that a huge, black mass manifested in the bedroom. Ed, who was in the home's occult museum at the time, witnessed a weird shadow figure that exuded a putrid, sickening smell. Ed began to pray and shouted out commands, telling the figure that it had to return to where it had come from in the name of Jesus Christ. The prayers seemed to work, and the figure vanished.

The story is one I can, personally, relate to. Through the years, there have been numerous occasions that I've been confronted by something disturbing and have called on prayer to get rid of dark manifestations. It's important to acknowledge these things, energetically speaking. Ignoring them will only give them more power and does not keep you safe. But when you do acknowledge them, you need to call on your faith to keep yourself protected. You need to focus your intent on driving the things away. For me, these are some of the key important elements when exploring and investigating the paranormal.

According to the Warrens, when they interviewed George Lutz, he was reluctant to talk much about the events that happened while his family lived in the house. Ed would ask the same question over and over, "What happened in the house, George?" The response from George would always be, "You know."

Reportedly, George was afraid to talk about the events because his family was still experiencing paranormal phenomena, even after leaving the home behind.

The Warrens weren't the only famous paranormal investigators to become involved with the Amityville case. As expected, DeFeo's lawyer, William Weber, delved deeply into the case for the trial. During this time, he became interested in some of the odd facts surrounding the murders. The focus of the defense was on the killer's mental state and condition, and even though the tactic wasn't successful in getting DeFeo off, there was a general acceptance of his psychiatric problems.

But Weber had a feeling there was something even stranger at work. Believing demonic forces could be at play, Weber contacted parapsychologist Hans Holzer. Holzer was well-known for his investigations into the supernatural, and Weber hoped Holzer could add a different perspective on the case.

Holzer agreed to look into the alleged incidents. When Holzer visited the house, he brought along a trance medium, Ethel Johnson Meyer. She had worked with Holzer on a number of occasions, and the parapsychologist was confident in her abilities.

Right away, Meyers began receiving impressions. She claimed the home had, indeed, been built on Native burial grounds. As a result of this, Meyers believed there were angry Native spirits on the property, walking the land and seeking revenge after having been disturbed.

I find Meyers' impressions very interesting. When Ronald DeFeo, Jr., was living in the house, he was said to have sudden, angry outbursts. He would also have moments where he went into trance-like states. Whether this was simply from drug use, or whether there was something else exerting an influence on him, is hard to say.

I do know that such manifestations can arise when demonic influences are trying to take someone over. Evil entities push into their victims' minds, bodies, and spirits, worming their way in more and more with each bit of effort. With his drug use and preexisting anger issues, DeFeo was a perfect vessel for evil.

During his investigation of the home, Holzer discovered bullet holes from the 1974 murders. He snapped photos of the holes as part of his documentation of the site. When the photos were developed, the pictures showed light anomalies around the bullet holes. The anomalies looked like halos of light over the holes.

While Holzer and Meyers were investigating the location, the trance medium had other impressions. She felt the spirits of the Defeo family were still present in the house. The DeFeos, she said, were consumed with a question: Why had they been killed by one of their own family members? She said the spirits in the home were overwhelmed with sadness and torment from the events that led to their deaths. Ethel Meyers did her best to cleanse the home and tried to help the spirits of the DeFeo family move on to the other side.

Just like many other people who became interested in the Amityville case, Hans Holzer was compelled to find out all he could about the events that had transpired in the home. Wanting to take his investigation further, Holzer arranged to meet with Ronald DeFeo, Jr., himself.

Holzer and DeFeo's attorney, Weber, went to the prison where DeFeo was incarcerated. Hoping to get more information, Holzer attempted to use hypnosis on DeFeo, but it wouldn't take. During the attempt, Ronald, Jr. responded saying how "they" wouldn't permit it to happen, meaning the hypnotic state. The big question, of course, was, who were "they?"

With hypnosis failing, Holzer decided to just interview Defeo. During their conversation, Ronald, Jr. told Holzer that he and his family had experienced supernatural events while living in the house in the time leading up to the murders.

Ronald, Jr. claimed they had heard unexplainable noises in the home. At one point, the entire family became convinced that they weren't the only people living in the house. According to Ronald, Jr., every family member had heard strange sounds, including phantom footsteps and knocking on the walls.

DeFeo further claimed that he had experienced things himself, including hearing blood-curdling screams when no one else was present. He also told Holzer that he recalled how his entire family discussed the unexplained events that were taking place. These events led to the DeFeos placing religious items throughout the home. Ronald, Jr.'s mother had sensed, what she believed to be, something evil in the home, and she believed having religious items placed throughout the house was the way to ward it off.

Ronald, Jr. also claimed that on the day of the murders, he fought with himself inside, trying to stop what was happening, but was unable to do so.

Was this due to his psychotic condition, or was it the result of some other outside influence? Some people have speculated that a disturbed and angry Native spirit took control of DeFeo, getting revenge for the house built on sacred land. As I mentioned previously, the story that haunted sites are built on burial grounds is a frequent claim. But in the case of the Amityville house, there really is something to the story.

The Amityville Historical Society dismissed the claims, but when Hans Holzer was involved with a documentary about the case, he interviewed a representative from the property development company who admitted that the house at 112 Ocean Avenue was, indeed, built on sacred burial grounds.

As I stated, I'd always heard stories about the Amityville haunting. Since I've always loved horror movies, I had seen "The Amityville Horror" when I was a kid. I thought it was a classic, creepy movie and enjoyed it. But it was a different ballgame when I was older and started doing paranormal investigations. Having witnessed a lot of strange things firsthand, I found myself again fascinated with the Amityville case. Living close to such a notorious and famous site, I couldn't help but want to learn more about the possible demonic connections to the story.

Additionally, after I learned what psychics like Lorraine Warren and Ethel Meyers had picked up about the case, I was interested in seeing what I could learn myself. Maybe I could add more to help complete the picture of what had happened inside the house.

I found myself going to the home frequently. The house is privately owned, and they don't open their doors for paranormal investigators, but I have found over time that the energy of the tragic events can easily be picked up on in the general area.

I've live-streamed a number of periscope broadcasts from

close proximity to the famous home. I also visited the cemetery where the DeFeo family is buried. It's in Farmingdale, about fifteen minutes from the house. It's a large cemetery, and it took some time to locate the graves. Standing at the DeFeo graves, I decided to do a live stream and see if I could communicate with the spirits of any of the family. Were they still lingering at the site of their final rest?

I started by asking if anyone from the DeFeo family was with me. I asked the question a few times, then got the name, John. I realized this was one of the children killed in 1974. Feeling like I was making contact, I dropped a big question and asked if a demon had influenced Ronald, Jr. in the murders of his family. I also asked if there had been a demon involved, and if so, what was its name? The device I was running responded with a name—Belial.

I knew the name. It was that of a demon found in both Hebrew and Christian demonology. The name itself means "wicked and worthless." Belial also means "ungodly." He is the personification of pride and lawlessness. Belial reigns as a king among demons and commands fifty legions. He is associated with people that are considered the lowest of humans or "the wicked men of the city" as they are called in the book of Judges.

The Dead Sea Scrolls mention Belial, naming him as an and angel of destruction and an important figure in the battle between the Sons of Light and the Sons of Darkness. Belial was said to be one of the original 666 fallen angels. As a prince of evil, he is a demon who opposes God's will every chance he gets. He overpowers humans and exerts his influence in the physical world. He lives in a dark domain, and his goal is to bring wickedness and guilt to the sons of man. Belial is a king of evil and has a terrifying countenance with a "visage like a viper." John Milton mentions Belial in book one of *Paradise Lost*:

"Belial came last, then whom a Spirit more lewd
Fell not from Heaven, or more gross to love
Vice for it self: To him no Temple stood

Or Altar smoak'd; yet who more oft then he
In Temples and at Altars, when the Priest
Turns Atheist, as did Ely's Sons who fill'd
With lust and violence the house of God."

Belial is destined to be defeated by God's armies led by the Archangel Michael. The demon will be chained and bound, ending its reign.

As humans, we are blessed with free will, the opportunity to make the right—or wrong—choices in the things we do. Our choices affect not just us but those around us in positive or negative ways.

Belial and other fallen angels fight against God over the creation of man. Because of this, they hate humans, and they hate the fact that we have free will. They try to use this against us and try to influence and corrupt humans at every opportunity.

It is important to understand just how dangerous these demons and devils are. Once they are invited in, or once they find an opening and begin to influence and oppress, they will not stop until they create endless suffering and torment. This is one of the ways they mock God and try to demonstrate that humans can't handle the responsibility of free will choice.

It was daylight when I did this brief session at the DeFeo gravesite. I didn't want to upset or disturb other people who were at the cemetery, visiting the graves of their loved ones, so I cut the session short and went back to my car.

I was parked very close to the DeFeo gravesites, sitting there thinking about what I had just picked up on and decided to see if the spirits would continue to communicate while I was parked there. I turned on a spirit box, a device that sweeps through radio frequencies, giving spirits an opportunity to use it to speak. I've had great success using spirit boxes and often found that the disembodied voices that come through offer direct responses to questions asked. This is a great way to get real-time responses during an investigation.

As soon as I turned the box on, I heard the voice of a little boy. It was so strange. I knew it was a young boy, but the tones were mumbled. I'd never heard anything like it before. It was also constant. This is also unusual since, usually, voices from a spirit box will be varied, as the departed use whatever tones are available that are being broadcasted. This was the same voice over and over, trying to communicate with me.

I thought about nine-year-old John, the boy killed by his older brother. It was his spirit that was believed to have been captured in the famous photograph inside the Amityville house. Was he still here? Was he the one trying so hard to speak with me?

I was cautious, as always. Demons can manifest in many forms and will often take the guise of humans, especially children, in order to make people vulnerable and open. But it was interesting that I had gotten the name, John, when I stood in front of the graves, and now what was clearly the voice of a young boy, trying to come through the spirit box.

Curious and cautious, I continued to try to communicate. I was praying to myself, keeping my protections up, and I asked the spirit, "Is this John? John, do you want me to say a prayer and try to help you?"

As soon as I asked the question, the voice of a little boy came through clearly on the box and responded, "Please." It was a single word, but it felt genuine, and it felt like there was emotion behind it.

The response was significant. Demons don't like the words of God, and they cannot stand prayers. Praying brings peace and brings a person closer to God, so it goes against everything that demons desire.

I visualized white light and said a prayer for the spirit of young John, hoping to at least give him some comfort and peace. I asked for the Archangel Michael to bring forth the light of the Holy Spirit and to bring peace to John and any other lost spirits that were around me at the time.

As always, it felt good calling out to higher spiritual powers, and it was a blessing to be able to offer at least something to any tormented souls that were stuck and not yet in heaven.

After I said the prayer, the little boy's voice continued to come through the spirit box. This was a little surprising to me. I always say that I can't and won't force spirits to cross over. I can only hope that they will do so after being offered prayers and light and encouraged to accept the path to God and heaven. Unconditional love and forgiveness go a long way, and often I feel like spirits have made the final journey after being offered help from this side. In this case, though, the little boy continued to mumble through the ghost box. The voice also sang out little words here and there in response to my questions and statements.

I made a decision while sitting there. I was going to the Amityville house itself. I would sit in my car near the home and see what kind of responses I could get being near the location of the murders.

From the cemetery, it was about a fifteen-minute drive to the house. I'll tell you, as soon as I turned on the street, there was a strange feeling. Maybe it's just me because I'm a sensitive, but an almost panicked feeling arose. It's like butterflies in your stomach, but more intense, nervous, and disturbing. I thought about the terrible crime, and I realized that Ocean Avenue, itself, is still permeated with the dark energy of the event.

I drove close enough to the house that I had a good view of it, and I parked my car. Over the years, the house has been altered. Some people who had owned the home didn't like the attention it had received from the famous movies. The iconic windows on the end of the house had been removed and changed, an attempt to obscure and change the home's history so that curiosity seekers couldn't spot it as easily. Physical appearances can be changed, but it isn't as easy to alter energy.

I turned on a spirit box again, hoping for more communication. I asked if there was anyone from the Amityville house there that would talk to me. Static noise came from the box, as it swept through frequencies, changing and jumping through channels.

I couldn't believe what happened next. A child's voice came

An unsettling feeling came over me as I drove down Ocean Avenue

through again! Once again, it was mumbling and making little noises. I was a fifteen-minute drive from the cemetery where this had just happened, yet it was the exact same voice coming out of the spirit box and was doing so in the same manner it had done when I was at the graves. I've never witnessed such a constant repetition of this level of response from the same voice, the same spirit, at different locations. It was stunning, and I knew that it was a rare moment.

I started asking questions, hoping to get detailed responses and information. I asked if anyone else was there, hoping that some spirit could manifest more clearly and give answers. But I continued to hear the same mumbling responses from the ghost box, and it was very difficult to distinguish specific words.

As the mumbling continued, I tried to pick out words and understand what the little boy wanted to say to me. Suddenly out of nowhere, another voice broke in and said a name clearly, "George."

Being a musician, I have a very good ear for sounds, voices, and accents. Not only was this voice extremely clear, but I could hear the accent in the voice. It was clearly a Long Island accent. This one was especially easy for me since I had lived in the area for so long, and I'm very familiar with the accent. I knew George Lutz was born on Long Island. Was he now trying to communicate with me?

George Lutz died in 2006, but because of the family's story and their experiences in the house, his name is forever associated with the Amityville story. Was he still connected to the location in spirit?

As I listened, more came from the spirit box.; it was as if a door had opened. A little boy's voice screamed out, "Ronnie!" and another voice said, "It's" or "They're coming."

I asked who was coming. There was so much pouring out from the box; it was as if the spirits were trying to talk over each other. A voice said, "shadow," leading me to wonder if shadow figures were being referred to, or if something else dark was meant. Was the little boy trying to warn me because I was asking questions?

I felt like something was holding the boy back, trying to prevent him from talking to me, trying to stop him from giving me information. I wondered to myself about the DeFeo father, Ronald, Sr. There had been stories and rumors that he was tied to the mob, and that he was an abusive person. None of this had been proven. And, of course, the man, himself, is not alive to defend his reputation. However, if he, or some other human spirit, was afraid of judgment, then it could be there holding the boy back, stopping him from giving me details. Maybe future investigations would give me more information; I would have to wait and see.

With so many strange responses, I decided to say some prayers to invoke peace. I started to pray, calling on Jesus Christ and the Blessed Mother. I called out loud, in the name of Jesus of Nazareth, in the name of the Blessed Mother, Virgin Mary, mother of God, angels and saints, help the spirit of this boy if he is stuck here. Whether it be his father or someone or something else, free him from evil.

I was still cautious and aware that this could well be something else and not a child at all. I have, many times, confronted evil spirits that tried using the voice of a child or other human to catch me off guard. But again, in this case, the voice of the boy had asked me to pray for him and asked for my help. No demonic entity would do that. It was very possible and likely that both the spirit of a young boy was there, as well as a dark, evil entity, be it a demon or something that was once human. In this case, there was something very evil and powerful present because all of my prayers weren't helping the spirit of the little boy.

The experience had been intense, and I left the location, driving home and trying to shake off the dark feelings associated with the house and whatever was still attached to it after so many years. I thought about the amount of time that had passed since the murders, but then considered that in the spirit realm, time is different. On that level, there is no concept of time as we know it, the past, the present, and the future are all one, so while it may not make sense in human terms that a demonic force still lingered at the Amityville home, in terms of spiritual understanding, it was no surprise. It was clear to me that forces of darkness were still present, below the surface, on Ocean Avenue.

As I sat at home thinking about the case, my mind raced over some of the synchronicities that I had noticed. When I had gone on the search for the DeFeo family graves, I discovered that they were buried in section 13 of the cemetery. This was weird because the date of the murders was November 13th. Furthermore, the Lutz family had moved into the home 13 months after the murders.

Numbers often have a symbolic and spiritual significance, and I tried to wrap my head around all the various connections with the number 13, the Lutz family, the DeFeos, and the Amityville house. Was it a sign of something more sinister at work?

Often, in demonic cases, there are notable connections with numbers, especially the number 13. Devils love to synchronize things, to create lines and symbols to intrigue and fascinate people to further draw them in. Often, if a human thinks they are making divine connections, their egos start to believe they are seeing God's patterns or messages from angels. But often, this is really something more sinister trying to play with a human's mind.

Many people in the paranormal field talk about these connections and try to understand exactly what it means and why malevolent entities like to do these things, but really, it's difficult to completely understand why they do. In some ways, it's like there's some kind of "demonic code," an underlying something that they use to further their goals.

Almost always, it seems to come back to an overall mockery of God and the Holy Trinity. For instance, in cases of demonic manifestation, people will often hear three knocks on the walls or doors, a mockery of the trinity.

I've dug into the symbology of the number thirteen in relation to the Bible and demonology, and I've found some interesting things. The number is symbolic of rebellion and lawlessness. The phrase "Valley of Hinnom" occurs in thirteen places in scripture. The valley was the scene of the evil inspired rites of the pagan god, Moloch or Molek. The practices related to this false god received some attention when they were, knowingly, allowed by King Solomon. As verse 1 Kings 11:7, says: *"On a hill east of Jerusalem, Solomon built a high place for Chemosh, the detestable god of Moab, and for Molek, the detestable god of the Ammonites."*

This was done by Solomon to please his non-Israelite wives. One of the ways Molech was appeased and worshiped was through the sacrifice of innocent children. They would be placed on the red-hot arms of the Moloch idol and burned alive. The valley's ties to fire made for an apt backdrop for the ultimate punishment of the unrepentant and rebellious sinners who ended up in the lake of fire in the book of Revelations. It's chapter 13 of Revelations that has one of the Bible's most well-known passages about evil: *"Let him that hath understanding count the number of the beast: for it is the number of a man; and his number is 666"* (Revelations 13:18).

Further reading of the Bible reveals other aspects of the number 13. Judas Iscariot was to be the 13th apostle, and his name is 13 letters long. Of course, in the Bible, Judas is the betrayer. When Jesus was asked who would betray him, he answered the question: *"Jesus answered, 'It is the one to whom I will give this piece of bread when I have dipped it in the dish.' Then, dipping the piece of bread, he gave it to Judas, the son of Simon Iscariot"* (John 13:16).

It's interesting to note that the betrayal is told of in chapter 13. The story continues in the same chapter as John tells about Judas showing up at the Garden of Gethsemane, where Jesus is praying. Judas and a mob of people, carrying swords and clubs, take Jesus and arrest him.

The next morning, Judas was supposedly consumed with guilt and remorse after what he had done, all for a handful of silver. The betrayer ended up hanging himself from a tree.

The name Judas has come up many times over the years during exorcisms, and some believe he has possessed people as a demon would do. Whether it is the spirit of Judas or demons using his name due to his famous betrayal is difficult to say.

Some of this was just the rambling curiosity of my mind, trying to make sense of all the connections that had started popping up in relation to the Amityville case. I wasn't surprised when all of this research into the number 13 ended up bringing me full circle to the demonic name I had heard while standing in the cemetery, trying to make connections with spirits from the house. Belial.

It was again, another chapter 13, this time the book of Deuteronomy that I read:

"Certain men, the children of Belial, are gone out from among you, and have withdrawn the inhabitants of their city, saying, Let us go and serve other gods, which ye have not known" (Deuteronomy 13:13).

Not only a thirteen, but a double thirteen, and a reference to Belial. Was I on to something, or was something trying to mock my work, toying with the spirits and me?

For me, the connections were clear and pure. They were direct from the Bible, the word of God, so I was confident in the information. Still, I couldn't make complete sense of it all; there were so many pieces and still so many unknowns.

All of this information continued to race about in my mind as I tried to make sense of the information and the various impressions I had about the Amityville house. A few nights later, I was still thinking about these things as I laid in bed, dozed off, and had a lucid dream.

I saw myself standing inside the Amityville house. I could see part of the first floor with a room to the left of the main staircase with a piano in the corner. As I looked up to the top of the first tier of stairs, I saw three clear shadow figures standing there. I didn't know who or what they were supposed to be.

I immediately thought about John DeFeo, the little boy who had been trying to make contact with me and whose voice I was sure I'd heard over the ghost box. I thought that John was trapped, held back by these three shadow figures that I now saw in the house. As I was staring at them, I yelled out at them, "In the name and authority of Jesus Christ of Nazareth, I command you to let this boy go if you're holding him back."

Right after I said this, the piano in the adjacent room was picked up by some invisible force and thrown at me. When the piano hit my body, I felt an electrical jolt in my bed that startled me awake.

I jumped up out of bed and saw a black, misty manifestation. The mass went through the ceiling above my bed. I immediately said a quick prayer of protection, knowing that there was something sinister about the figure.

I looked at my phone and found that the time was 3:15 a.m. The exact time of the murders of the DeFeo family and the time that George Lutz kept waking up each night during his time in the house.

I sat there shocked, thinking about the synchronicity and the lucid dream I had about being in the house. Was some force upset that I was praying for the souls connected to the horrific murders? I had now said several prayers for the spirit I believed to be that of young John DeFeo, and it appeared that I had angered something. What was their intent? How far would these forces go to stop me or attack me? I knew that I needed to be more careful and cautious in continuing to look into the demonic force associated with the Amityville house. I would, in fact, need to be even more on guard than ever. I felt the presence of this thing, and I knew that it could be extremely powerful.

The next weekend, I decided to go to Connecticut and investigate at a haunted cemetery. A friend of mine named Melissa was going with me. Little did I know what was to come.

Melissa has some natural psychic abilities. I knew it would be interesting to see what she picked up on, to see if it aligned with what I sensed and to see what would be different. While we were in the cemetery, we were live streaming on my periscope. At one point, Melissa suddenly gave me a warning. She said that "something really dark was watching me from the woods next to the cemetery." This is a testimony from Melissa giving her view of what happened that day:

"We got to the cemetery, and our moods went from

A vision of shadow figures at the Amityville house

spirited and curious to feeling completely irritated, quiet, and serious. Then we started wandering off in different directions toward some woods on the outskirts of the cemetery. Then, I went into complete hunting dog mode. I felt like we were being watched from the woods. That's when I told Sean to be careful, to protect his energy, and be on guard because the dark mass of energy there gave me the impression and feeling of wanting to challenge Sean and catch him off guard when he least expected it.

"After I warned Sean about what was happening, I felt like I was being put into a trance. I, personally, felt like it was enticing me to go in the woods by myself so it could separate us. I did go a bit into the woods, but then I snapped out of whatever was pulling me in. Then, I started feeling lightheaded, and I realized Sean wasn't around me. I started trying to make my way back to him, and I called his name two times, but he couldn't hear me.

"We found each other after a few minutes, and I told Sean that I was worried about how we had been acting. I kept asking him if he was ok. He seemed quiet and distant. Sean said he was fine, but that he felt off.

"We started walking, and when we did, we both noticed these flies. One by one, they were starting to gather around Sean. Not one of them were flying around me, even though we were close to each other. It didn't make sense because it was actually cool that day, so they shouldn't have been swarming at all. The live viewers on Sean's periscope were worried, too, and thought that we weren't acting like ourselves.

"Then, Sean and I both heard a sound from the spirit box. It was a loud, long guttural growl, and it happened just as the flies were swarming all around. Even the viewers on the live stream could see the flies."

As Melissa stated, the energies were strange that day, but the demonic growl wasn't the only thing that came out of the box. Standing there in a Connecticut cemetery, investigating a completely different site not associated with the Amityville house, I was given a reminder that dark entities aren't bound by physical location. Once they knew you were looking into their activity, they would pay attention to what you were doing. The spirit box said very clearly, "Amityville Belial."

I'm thinking you have to be f*#@ing kidding me! Is this really what's coming at me right now? Was this thing trying to attack me or intimidate me? Was it going to start intruding on any paranormal investigation that I was doing now, no matter where I was?

I knew this was a turning point, and that whatever this thing was, it was not going to leave me alone. The visions and experiences related to Amityville were going to continue in the weeks to come.

Another thing happened during this time. I found that I would automatically look at my phone every day at 3:15. It was never thought out. I was never trying to look at my phone and hit that time; it just kept happening.

Soon I had another experience. I was in bed and had fallen asleep when I found myself back in the Amityville house. This time, a black dog was there. This black dog was barking at the wall in the corner of a room in the house. There were clocks everywhere. The clocks all started going off—they were all set at 3:15 a.m. With the clocks all going off and the dog still barking at the corner of the room, a huge, black misty manifestation came out of the wall and came towards me.

I jumped up out of bed again. Just like on the previous occasion, I saw the black form go up through the ceiling over my bed. I looked at my cell phone. Yes, it was 3:15 a.m.

Standing there in the early morning hour, I had such a profound sense of dread. I could feel the negative presence that had been in my room and tried to attack me in my vision. The whole thing was very worrisome, but I always resort to my faith. I wasn't going to let this thing trigger fear and negative emotions within me. It made sense the thing was trying to come at me while I slept since it would be the time that I would be the most vulnerable. It was trying to exert its dark influence and fear on me.

Whatever this thing was, it continued to be a presence that

In front of the famous Long Island house

tried to get to me. The following weekend, I was at another haunted cemetery. Walking around, trying to make contact with spirits, I started to get the feeling of something very oppressive and evil. I received a very clear image of something physical nearby. The impression was of a black-cloaked figure that was following me. Again, flies started to swarm around me. I called on the authority of Jesus Christ and told the thing that it did not have permission to attack me. I could feel the thing become disempowered, and it started to dissipate. The heavy feelings stopped.

I had another strong impression about the murders of the DeFeo family. I believed that somehow, at least some of those souls were trapped and suffering. Here I was, trying my best to free the spirit of the little boy connected to the house. I had angered some devil just for trying to help a soul return to God. The demonic sees this as offensive, and they wanted to get back at me. More psychic experiences related to the Amityville house soon came. This time, I was astral projecting when the incident occurred.

Astral projection is when your soul leaves your physical body, usually while you're asleep, in a lucid dream-like experience. The soul remains attached to the physical body by a silver cord. I'd had such experiences many times over the years. It's something that a lot of people experience, but many people don't understand what is happening.

On this occasion, I found myself looking down at the Amityville house. It was like a bad documentary video. I was looking down at the home from about 50 to 60 feet above it. I saw the entire property; it was like looking at it from a drone's perspective.

What was unsettling about the experience was what I was hearing while looking down at the house. I heard a buzzing sound that I soon realized was the swarming of flies. They were buzzing in my ears, and it seemed like there were thousands of them. There were so many that the buzzing sound was deafening. The loud swarming of the flies overwhelmed me, and my body shook in my bed. It took me several seconds before I could wake up and come back into my body.

I woke up, jumping up in my bed. Yet again, I saw the manifestation of a black mist going up through the ceiling above my bed. By this time, it should come as no surprise that a glance at my phone verified that it was 3:15 a.m.

The synchronicities continued. I kept picking up my phone during the day at exactly 3:15, and I kept feeling the dark presence that was connected to the house, even though I had not returned to the property or even the cemetery where the DeFeo family was buried. My initial investigations had been enough to put me on the radar of something demonic.

Another night, another vision came. I found myself standing in front of the boathouse behind the home. The door was creaking open as I watched. I started to walk in to see if someone was inside. I peeked in, and I could see a dark shadow figure in a completely dark room. This may seem like it makes no sense, but the figure was blacker than darkness, blacker than the room in its natural darkness. I asked out loud, "Is that you, George?" "George Lutz?"

Again, I woke up. A glance at my phone showed the expected time, 3:15 a.m. This time, however, there was no black mist, no manifestation darting up through the ceiling. I sat down and wondered what this latest vision meant and how it fit in with the other information I had been getting about the house. Was the spirit of George Lutz still in the home or attached to it somehow?

I thought about Ed and Lorraine Warren and how they had said the case was so profound for them, and that it stayed with them. The Amityville house case is like glue. Every time someone gets involved and starts probing into it, something about it sticks to the person, and it's hard, almost impossible to shake off. Once the connection starts, it keeps going, and things start to happen.

I wanted to talk to someone about the case to get another perspective and opinion, and I knew exactly who to speak with. Ralph Sarchie.

Ralph Sarchie is a well-respected demonologist. He worked with the Warrens and was, himself, mentored by the most respected exorcists of our time, Bishop McKenna and Father Malachi Martin. I'm fortunate to have been mentored by Ralph, who taught me so much about demonology. I've gone on a lot of cases with Ralph and was even lucky enough to end up on his pilot series, *The Demon Files*, for three episodes.

Ralph has a plethora of knowledge, and it's been a humbling experience to learn from him, especially considering his knowledge of dark and demonic entities. Ralph is a real spiritual warrior and knows that the devil and his minions are all too real.

He's also familiar with the Amityville case. I went out to Long Island one evening to visit Ralph and talk to him about the case, and some of my experiences related to it. Talking about spiritual matters with Ralph is always intense and educational. I love hearing about his personal experiences from all the years he has investigated the paranormal as a demonologist.

I told Ralph about the things that had happened since I had started looking into the Amityville murders and the demonic energy connected to the house. Ralph agreed that no demonic entity would ever want prayer for any reason. This confirmed my belief that the boy spirit was not a demon in disguise. Between the confirmation and conversation with Ralph, I found myself wanting to go back to the house to see if I could get more information and communication.

I asked Ralph if he wanted to go to the house that night. "Sean, you're asking me to go play with the devil tonight?" he replied. I laughed and told him to take it any way he wanted to. Ralph responded, "I don't want you to go over there alone at night. Let's take a ride over there."

Pulling onto Ocean Avenue always gives me a sense of panic and pressure. I could feel it in my chest, intense and a bit scary. We pulled over into a parking space not far from the house. I turned on a ghost box to see if we could get any responses. I used an auxiliary cable and hooked the device up to my car radio so responses could come through the car's speakers.

Once again, the voice of a little boy started to come through.

As we asked questions, we started getting relevant responses. Between the responses from the little boy, there was something else, a snarling sound that pressed in as if it didn't want the boy to respond. We asked whatever was communicating if it could mimic and project the sound of the gunshot from that night in 1974.

BOOM! The sound came out loud from the car speakers. It sounded just like a gunshot, and it shook the whole car because it was so loud. Ralph and I looked at each other in shock.

After a moment, I asked another question, something that had been on my mind for some time. "John, was that you in the photograph taken in the house by the Warren team's photographer?" The little boy's voice responded, "It wasn't me."

The response was interesting to me. Even though many people have noted the similarity between the Lutz boy and the ghostly image in the photo, Ed Warren himself had stated in an interview that he didn't believe the photo was John Lutz. Rather, Ed thought it was something diabolical in nature.

Ralph was surprised by the responses we were getting that night. When we left, we went over everything that had happened, along with the experiences I'd had since I started looking into the case.

Ralph agreed that the little boy could be trapped in the home, held there by something dark. The next time he was at Mass, Ralph gave up his communion and prayed to the Lord for mercy on the boy, hoping the boy could find peace if he was truly there.

During my conversation with Ralph about the Amityville case, he told me that George was sometimes referred to by his middle name, Lee. After hearing this information, the name Lee started to pop up during some of my investigations. It seemed, in fact, that the spirit of George Lutz was actively trying to connect with me and communicate.

I continued to wake up at 3:15 a.m. every morning. One morning, I woke up and saw an image of George's face. I heard his voice, too. "That was my house," he stated.

His name kept coming up when I was doing investigations, even ones not connected in any way to the Long Island house. These experiences unfolded over several years though they lessened somewhat over time. When I was working on the draft for this book, Amityville references started to come in again.

While filming the series, "Ghost Loop," for the Travel Channel, the presence of the Amityville spirits would make themselves present in my life once more.

We were in Houston, Texas, investigating a case in the area for an episode of the show. Funny enough, I had spoken to one of the girls working at the front desk at the hotel about what we were doing in the area. She told me there was talk of the hotel being haunted; and that it had been an apartment complex before it was a hotel.

I was excited that not only were we in the area for a case, but the hotel we were in was also haunted. I decided to do a live stream in my room to see if I could find out who or what was haunting the hotel. Towards the end of my live stream, I clearly saw the image of a face. It was George Lutz. I asked the spirit box, "George, is that you? Are you here with me right now?" The response from the box was clear, "Lutz." "Why would you be following me?" I asked. The responses that came from the box made it clear, "Chapter . . . Amityville took my soul."

Once again, I couldn't believe the responses and connections. The Amityville case is really haunting in more than one sense. If George said that it took his soul, that could mean a lot of different things. Either way, it was very unsettling and disturbing.

I was on the road for two months, working on "Ghost Loop." When I got back home, I set myself to work on this book. Once again, Amityville was on my mind. I thought about all the experiences, information, and visions—the startling experience that Ralph and I had had outside the house. Had my prayers and the spiritual work that Ralph had done helped the little boy? Was he finally free?

I decided to go back to the house to see if I would still get responses from any spirits there. I returned to the DeFeo family gravesite first and turned on a ghost box to see if I could make contact. I asked if we had helped John. A voice came from the box that said, "It's over."

The answer had only come after I asked the question several times. It seemed to me that the spirits were having a difficult time communicating, and it was hard for me to get confirmation while I was there. I said some prayers and headed home. I was tired and decided to take a quick day nap. When I did, I received a vision.

I saw a little boy standing in front of me. He was covered with water. His face was pale, and he had a dead stare. The boy uttered, "I drowned." Even his voice sounded dead and cold. Then, he started to moan in slow bits. It was a long moan, and it got louder and louder as it continued. As the moans increased in volume, I saw a pair of yellow, glowing eyes over the boy's left shoulder. Beyond that, there was another set of glowing eyes that were watching from afar. I had the sense that whatever it was, it was in control of the scene I was seeing. Was this a demonic manifestation? Was something mocking the drowning of a boy?

After the vision, I asked around to see if there was any talk of a drowning near the Amityville house. Although hard to confirm, there are stories that a boy drowned somewhere near the property in the early 1900s.

I'm not sure what, exactly, this vision was all about. It seemed to be another scare tactic from some dark force. Perhaps something was mocking the boy's death and trying to show its power.

There was a cold chill in my room when I had the experience. I immediately blessed my room and said some prayers. I was, again, reminded that something was not happy that I had gotten involved with the Amityville case. My attempts to help spirits connected to the case put me on their radar. Despite that, I was still curious about John and wondered if he had received the help he needed. I decided to take another drive to Ocean Avenue.

As I had done before, I parked near the house and started

up a device to make contact. I asked if any spirits still resided in the home. "Death," was the response from the box. In fact, the ghost box said this same word several times. I asked again if we had been able to help the boy, John. The response was, "You helped him."

Obviously, I can't prove this for sure, but I've now gone back to the house several times, and the boy's voice has never returned on the spirit box. I have received several verifications that we were, indeed, able to help him cross over. All of this, together, leads me to feel like we were successful in helping John.

While I was working on writing down these accounts, I posted on my social media that I was working on telling my story of personal connections and experiences with the famous horror house. A gentleman contacted me to share his own experiences. He'd been researching the case for fifteen years. He told me that during his time studying the case, he'd started corresponding with another man who claimed to have purchased the actual negatives of the crime scene at an auction.

After the man bought the negatives and took them home, he started to experience disturbing activity in his house. He started waking up with nightmares every night. Looking at his clock, it turned out that he was waking up at 3:15 a.m., the time of the murders.

My correspondent told me that the man had sent him copies of the crime scene images. Out of nowhere, he, too, started having nightmares. He, too, started waking up at the murder time. Despite having researched the case himself for years, he decided to stop corresponding with the owner of the negatives. When he did, the nightmares stopped, and the strange activity ceased. He later learned that the man who had purchased the crime scene negatives had hung himself.

I asked my correspondent if he would write down some notes about his experiences looking into the Amityville case. At first, he agreed to do so, but when he started writing his experiences down, the nightmares quickly returned. He was very apprehensive about continuing, so I told him not to worry about it. I fully understood what it was like to be plagued by the energies of the house and the murders.

I did continue to correspond with him, and he told me other things. Reportedly, a young man who lived in the home, sometime after the Lutz family, had died of an overdose in the house. It's said he was sleeping in Ronald DeFeo, Jr.'s bedroom. If true, it's a strange coincidence, considering DeFeo's drug use.

Of course, I can't testify to the absolute truth of my correspondent's story; however, considering my own experiences, while looking into the case, I tend to believe what he told me.

Messaging back and forth with this man also induced another vision about the house. The first night I received information from him, I dreamed I was standing in front of the house. There was a girl in a white nightgown in front of me, right in my face, screaming bloody murder.

I woke up suddenly, startled. It was, of course, 3:15 a.m.

Simply writing about the Amityville case and my experiences connected to it has caused a resurgence of activity around me that I associate with the spirits and demonic forces involved.

I recalled the experience I wrote about in my first book that involved the house. It was a vision of being in the backseat of a car with Lorraine Warren. I could tell from her plaid skirt that it was the 1970s. Ed Warren was driving, and he took a quick look at us and said, "We're off to Amityville."

We arrived at the house and went inside. Ed took me aside and said, "Sean, you know we are back in time now." I replied, "Really?"

He told me I was a big part of this and that I should take a look upstairs. When I looked up, I saw the word "accolade" floating in front of the stairs on the second floor. I wondered for a long time what the word meant for me in this case. After my experiences with the spirit of young John DeFeo, I'd wondered if the word was an acknowledgment that I would help the boy's spirit find peace.

During the course of working on this book, I continued to investigate various haunted locations. Once, while live streaming with a spirit box, I heard a voice come through that clearly stated, "I'm in prison."

Now, as I've stated before, having been a musician for so many years, I have a very good ear for sound and voices. Usually, once I hear a voice a few times, I will recognize it when I hear it again. This particular voice sent a chill through me because I recognized it. It sounded like Ronald DeFeo, Jr.

I even told the live stream audience that the voice sounded like DeFeo. DeFeo is, of course, in prison and not deceased. Why was his voice coming through a ghost box when I was doing something completely unattached to the Amityville home? Was this something demonic imitating his voice, knowing that I was likely to recognize it?

When I got home, I clipped the phrase out of my audio recording and spliced it together with audio from an interview with Ronald, Jr. Running the audio back-to-back, there was no doubt. The raspy, Long Island accent and its inflection made it clear to me—the voice that had come over my ghost box that night was that of Ronald DeFeo, Jr.

Honestly, I'm not sure what the purpose or intent of this was. It's one of many examples of how the case still haunts me to this day. Once you get involved with the Amityville story, something about it attaches to you, and it doesn't let go. It gets into your head and your spirit.

On a regular basis, I have visions related to the case. I hear the names of key people involved come over the ghost box. I hear the number 112, the address of the house, and at times, I still wake up at 3:15 a.m., the moment of the murders.

Even now, writing about this case, I'm hearing the buzzing of flies, but it's cold, and there are no flies around me, at least not physically.

I know a lot of people still believe the entire thing was just a story, a hoax carried out to make money from movies, but here's a fact: Ronald DeFeo, Jr. carried out a series of horrible murders in his family's home on Long Island. He left an entire family dead, all in the same position, and there's no real explanation for how or why he did it.

You can put it down to psychotic behavior, drugs, or any other excuse, but the event left a mark on the house in Amityville. To this day, there's a darkness that still swirls around the story. The house sits there, quietly, but it has an evil stain on it, and no matter what people believe, I know there is something diabolical there, still lurking in the shadows and waiting for the next opportunity to get someone in its clutches.

If you choose to look at the Amityville case, be careful, something will look back, and you may not want its attention.

Giving Thanks

This year, 2020, as I work on my second book, I realize that it's been over a decade since I became involved in the paranormal. Since that time, every single day of my life, I have experienced something related to the spiritual realm. It hasn't been without its challenges, but I wouldn't give any of it back. I understand and am humbled by the gifts that God has given me that help guide me along my path. At times, it's a very dark path, but I always try to keep focused on my inner light, and keep my faith, remaining as spiritually strong as I can. I hope that my spiritual mission continues to bring light and that I'm accomplishing what my soul and my higher self are here to do.

There are many individuals that I've been blessed to know who have helped me along on my journey, so I'd like to offer a few special thanks:

Thanks to my mentor in demonology Ralph Sarchie. Since our first meeting, it's been a blessing to learn from Ralph and the experiences with him have been incredible. God bless Ralph and his continued work.

Thanks to my coauthor David Weatherly for turning these accounts into a professional creation. I've done many investigations with David and his extensive knowledge of the paranormal always makes for a fascinating trip.

Thank you to Sam Shearon for bringing my visions to life with his fantastic cover art. I'm always amazed by Sam's talent.

Thanks to Kimberly Carper for the drawings of my experiences. The visuals are both fantastic and chilling.

Thanks to Kamra Images for the great photos used in the book. Always great to work with such pros.

A Special thanks to Ed Warren. Ed passed away in 2006 and I now believe he is a guide of some sort helping me along the way from above. The first demonology book I ever read was one written by Ed and I have long felt his influence in my life.

Thanks to everyone who shared their experiences for this book. It's surreal to be in this position, writing my second book, and each of your contributions has helped tremendously.

And finally, I want to thank each and every one of you who have taken the time to read this book and have been a part of my path along the way. You have all been a defining part of my spiritual journey.

About the Authors

Sean Austin

Feeling a spiritual connection to music from an early age, Sean started playing music and taught himself several instruments by the time he was a teenager. He has written and recorded original music and performed as an opening act for numerous bands around the country.

Sean's music has been called "emotional and genuine" in the vein of Pearl Jam and the Goo Goo Dolls.

His acclaimed CD, "Shapeshifter," was released in 2017.

When a series of strange experiences led him to delve into the world of the paranormal, he found his second passion—exploring the unknown and the afterlife.

A lifelong Catholic, Sean believes his faith and religious views are the key components in his pursuit to understand the world beyond and communicate with spirits. His time in the paranormal helped open latent psychic abilities that he continues to explore and develop.

Sean Austin was also a cast member on Destination America's three-episode show, "Demon Files," where he worked with his mentor, well-known demonologist Ralph Sarchie. Sean later starred in the Travel Channel show "Ghost Loop."

Between music gigs, he continues to explore haunted locations around the country.

Find Sean online at:

https://seandaustin.com/

David Weatherly

David Weatherly is a renaissance man of the strange and supernatural. He has traveled the world in pursuit of ghosts, cryptids, UFOs, magic, and more. From the specters of dusty castles to remote, haunted islands, from ancient sites to modern mysteries, he has journeyed to the most unusual places on the globe seeking the unknown.

David became fascinated with the paranormal at a young age. Ghost stories and accounts of weird creatures and UFOs led him to discover many of his early influences. Writers such as John Keel, Jacques Vallee, Hans Holzer, and others set him on course to spend his life exploring and investigating the unexplained.

Throughout his life, he's also delved into shamanic and magical traditions from around the world, spending time with elders from numerous cultures in Europe, the Americas, Africa, and Asia. He has studied with Taoist masters in China, Tibetan Lamas, and other mystics from the Far East. He's picked up knowledge from African and Native American tribal elders and sat around fires with shaman from countless other traditions.

Along his path, David has also gathered a lot of arcane knowledge, studying a range of ancient arts from palmistry, the runes, and other obscure forms of divination, to alchemy and magick. He has studied and taught Qigong and Ninjutsu, as well as various energy-related arts. David has also studied stage and performance magic.

His shamanic and magical backgrounds have given him unique perspectives in his explorations into the unknown, and he continues to write, travel, and explore, leaving no stone unturned in his quest for the strange and unusual.

David has investigated, and written about, a diverse range of topics, including Hauntings & Ghosts, Cryptozoology, Ufology, Ancient Mysteries, Shamanism, Magic, and Psychic Phenomena.

David is the founder of the independent media and publishing company, Eerie Lights Publishing.

He has been a featured speaker at conferences around the world and has lectured for countless paranormal and spiritual groups.

He is a frequent guest on Coast to Coast AM with George Noory, Spaced Out Radio, and other radio programs. David has also appeared on numerous television shows, including the Travel Channel's "Mysteries of the Outdoors," History Channel's "Ancient Aliens," "Beyond Belief," and other programs. He was also featured in the highly successful series, "On the Trail of UFOs."

David's books include Strange Intruders, Black Eyed Children, and the Cryptid States series.

Find David online at:

https://eerielights.com/

Made in USA - North Chelmsford, MA
1180285_9781945950209
10.13.2020 1626